LIFE WORLD LIBRARY

SPAIN

LIFE WORLD LIBRARY

SPAIN

by Hugh Thomas
and The Editors of LIFE

TIME INCORPORATED . NEW YORK

COVER: Two small boys
chat among the simple,
sun-bathed houses of Avila,
a centuries-old town in Castile,
not far from Madrid.

ABOUT THE WRITER

Hugh Thomas, who wrote the interpretive chapters for this volume of the
LIFE World Library, is a British author whose meticulous and massive history, *The Spanish Civil War*, published in 1961, was acclaimed by critics
as the first balanced and thorough story of that conflict. He has also written two novels, *The World's Game* and *The Oxygen Age*. A graduate of
Cambridge, he was president of that university's ancient debating society,
the Union, and received a first (equivalent of an American *summa cum
laude*) in history. He later spent a year in further study at the Sorbonne in
Paris and another two years working in the British Foreign Office. He re-
signed from the Foreign Office to devote his time to writing and has since
traveled widely in Spain.

Spain © 1962, 1966 by Time Inc. All rights reserved. Published simultaneously in Canada.
Library of Congress catalogue card number 62-20648.
School and library distribution by Silver Burdett Company.

Contents

TIME-LIFE BOOKS

EDITOR
Maitland A. Edey
TEXT DIRECTOR   ART DIRECTOR
Jerry Korn   Edward A. Hamilton
CHIEF OF RESEARCH
Beatrice T. Dobie
Assistant Text Director: Harold C. Field
Assistant Art Director: Arnold C. Holeywell
Assistant Chiefs of Research:
Monica O. Horne, Martha Turner

•

PUBLISHER
Rhett Austell
General Manager: Joseph C. Hazen Jr.
Planning Director: Frank M. White
Business Manager: John D. McSweeney
Circulation Director: Joan D. Manley
Publishing Board: Nicholas Benton, Louis Bronzo,
James Wendell Forbes, John S. Wiseman

LIFE MAGAZINE

EDITOR: Edward K. Thompson
MANAGING EDITOR: George P. Hunt
PUBLISHER: Jerome S. Hardy

LIFE WORLD LIBRARY

SERIES EDITOR: Oliver E. Allen
Editorial Staff for *Spain:*
Text Editors: Hillis Mills, Norton Wood
Designer: Ben Schultz
Staff Writers: David S. Thomson, John Stanton
Chief Researcher: Grace Brynolson
Researchers: Irene Ertugrul, Paula von Haimberger Arno,
Edward Brash, Mollie Cooper, Renée Pickèl, Louise Samuels,
Helen R. Turvey, Ava Weekes, Linda Wolfe

EDITORIAL PRODUCTION
Color Director: Robert L. Young
Copy Staff: Marian Gordon Goldman, Barbara Hults,
Dolores A. Littles
Picture Bureau: Margaret K. Goldsmith, Joan Lynch
Traffic: Douglas B. Graham
Art Assistant: Gretchen Cassidy

Valuable assistance in the preparation of this book was given by the
following individuals and departments of Time Inc.: Dmitri Kessel,
LIFE staff photographer; Thomas Dozier, former Chief of the Madrid
Bureau; Joaquín Segura of LIFE EN ESPAÑOL; Doris O'Neil, Chief of
the LIFE Picture Library; Richard M. Clurman, Chief, TIME-LIFE News
Service; and Peter Draz, Chief of the Bureau of Editorial Reference.

Introduction

The famous Spanish writer José María Giro-nella says in the preface to his novel *The Cypresses Believe in God,* "Spain is an unknown country. Experience proves that it is hard to view my country impartially. Even writers of high order succumb to the temptation to adulterate the truth, to treat our customs and our psychology as though everything about them were of a piece, of a single color. Legends and labels pile up: black Spain, inquisitorial Spain, beautiful Spain, tragic Spain, folkloric Spain, unhappy Spain, a projection of Africa into the map of Europe."

The present volume, written by the British author Hugh Thomas, contains much useful information and perceptive insights into the character of the people of this storied land. It also presents some observations and judgments on which there will be honest differences of opinion. If this book throws light into dark places and provokes responsible discussion, it will serve our common cause.

A realization which I have found helpful in understanding Spain and its political traditions is that this ancient land, located on the edge of Europe and associated for several hundred years with North African peoples, was influenced only very slightly by two of the philosophical experiences which are fundamental to the origin of our country and of our way of thinking. I refer to the profound changes in thought which grew out of 18th Century rationalism and the French Revolution.

Similarly, the impact of the 19th Century industrial revolution upon Spain's economic and social fabric was not nearly so far-reaching as in other countries of western Europe, in Great Britain or in the United States.

Moreover, Spain was never exposed to the Protestant Reformation, surely one of the most significant upheavals of modern history. Indeed, Spain was the source, the center and the motive power of the Counter Reformation.

Finally, it should be remembered, as Mr. Thomas points out, that almost all of Spain was occupied for many centuries by the Moors, with results that persist to the present day. Yet, during the past few years, individual Spaniards and Americans have worked closely together in a fruitful relationship founded on mutual respect and on the larger concept of the defense of the western world against the onslaught of Communist imperialism.

There is a magic and a mystery in Spain that challenges our understanding. Spain is a land of stoics and mystics, of poets and painters, of dreamers and realists. The capacity of the noble Spanish people for loyal friendship, their courage, their concept of the dignity of the individual are characteristics that command respect and inspire affection.

Unity is the greatest element in our entire arsenal of power. Spain, which has contributed so much to western culture, must be a part of that unity. United, even at this late hour, we can emerge from the dark clouds which are charging down upon us and into the sunlight of a secure peace.

JOHN DAVIS LODGE
former U.S. Ambassador to Spain

1

New Stirrings
in an
Ancient Land

IN Madrid, once among the quietest of Western Europe's capitals, the traffic each day is bumper to bumper on downtown streets. In Seville and Valladolid, remembered by visitors as sleepy provincial municipalities, dozens of modern factories have risen to house the whirring machines of industry. In Palomares and Marbella and all the other towns along the sunny Costa del Sol, which only yesterday were being "discovered" by knowledgeable travelers as unspoiled old-world retreats, tourists by the million jam the beaches all summer long. And in the tiny *pueblos* or villages of Spain, where indoor plumbing is unheard of and donkeys still roam the streets, the peasants cluster at night in the local *tabernas* to watch American soap operas on television.

Spain has taken a sudden plunge into the 20th Century.

The Spanish nation was isolated from most of Europe—and indeed most of the world—by its political coloration after the Civil War of 1936-1939. In that grim conflict, Generalissimo Francisco Franco triumphed over his Republican enemies with material help from Hitler and Mussolini. To govern Spain he set up a police state on the Fascist model. After the downfall of his ideological partners in Germany and Italy in World War II, Franco and his chosen officials never changed their convictions about the necessity for one-party government based on "total" discipline of the masses. Instead they withdrew into a mood of self-righteousness and xenophobia. For two decades Spain rocked along under the control of aging generals and admirals scornful of individual liberty, fearful of contamination by any "progressivism" that might threaten their established order, and sullenly defiant toward the outside world.

NOW another generation is making its influence felt in the national life, a generation less committed to the old ideas of absolutism and sometimes receptive to change. The dictatorship, after long years of secure power, now wears an air of benevolence more often than repression. At the same time hostility toward Spain has abated somewhat beyond the Pyrenees. Today in defense arrangements, in economic affairs and in diplomacy, Spain has emerged from the lonely isolation of the postwar years to become identified increasingly with the prospering community of Western nations.

The reasons for this emergence and some of its consequences will be examined in later chapters of this book. But first, who are the Spanish people and what are they like?

Through the course of history the land area of present-day Spain has been occupied by many different tribes of men. Spanish blood is an exotic mixture of strains contributed by early Mediterranean and African peoples as well as North Europeans. The Spanish national character evolved during eight centuries of Roman and Gothic rule followed by eight centuries of struggle against the Moors—Moslem invaders from Africa and Asia—and three centuries as a great Christian empire which had the power to extend its language and culture through much of the modern world.

The Spaniard today is proud, individualistic, complex. His pride is that natural pride observed by the French historian Brantôme when he marveled at the Spanish soldiers riding to quell an uprising in Flanders in their "arrogant and insolent grace." It is the self-esteem (mixed with a wry fatalism) suggested by an ancient Spanish parable: "When God created Spain, He allowed the Spaniards three wishes. They chose to have the most varied climate in the world, the most beautiful women and the most delicious foods and fruit and wine, and God agreed. But after a bit they came back with a fourth wish: to have a good government. And God said, 'That is too much to ask.'"

Spaniards like to tell this kind of story, and afterward they may shrug and murmur with satisfaction: *"muy español"* (very Spanish).

THE Spaniard's independence of spirit has been described variously as egoism, rebelliousness and mulish inability to compromise; an American social scientist defines this quality as "contrariety, the habit of being *against* things." Officials of the Franco regime tend toward the view that the Spaniard is too much of an anarchist by natural inclination to be entrusted with self-government, and must be ruled with a firm hand.

The exiled Spanish historian Salvador de Madariaga writes of his countrymen's "anticooperative instinct," and explains it in terms of the religious training that encourages a concentration on one's individual relationship to God. "Whether consciously or not," observes Madariaga, "the Spaniard lives against a background of eternity, and his outlook is more religious than philosophic."

The Spaniard may remark, with a touch of pride, "We are the impossible people." He may say furiously, with no particular political ax to grind and no solution to offer, "It is one of the evils of Spain. We are corrupt and priest-ridden (or decadent or ungovernable)." The Spaniard is his own severest critic, but that does not mean that he will accept criticism from anyone else. The Spanish people are deeply resentful of what they call *la leyenda negra* (the black legend)—an old term that includes any derogatory sentiment expressed by foreigners about Spain ("The Spanish are cruel," "The Spanish

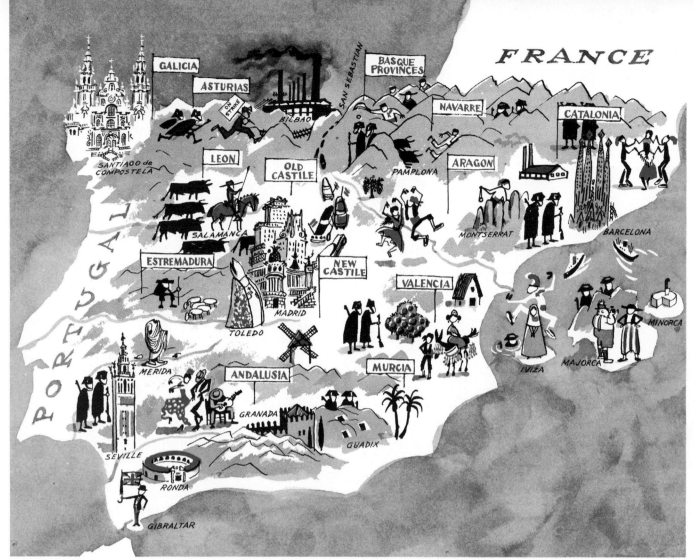

THE LIVELY DIVERSITY of Spain is shown above in an artist's conception of the country's regions. Characteristic peoples or famous products and landmarks—like the Basque *jai alai* players or Minorca's cheese—appear with each region. Everywhere there are the country's black-hatted, rifle-carrying policemen, the Guardia Civil.

exploited their American colonies," etc., etc.).

The Spaniard is contradictory and inclined to go to extremes. He is either elaborately garrulous or gloomily silent, violently animated or coldly indifferent. He sees things as either black or white, heaven or hell, an agony or an ecstasy. A visitor to the country is conscious of the brilliant sunshine that constantly recalls the pure joy of living, and yet the Spaniard appears to be morbidly preoccupied with the idea of death.

The English novelist and critic V. S. Pritchett has said in his brilliant book *The Spanish Temper* that he is "frankly frightened" when he visits Spain, "the old and necessary enemy of the West. There we learn our history upside down and see life exposed to the skin. . . . All the hungers of life are blankly stated there. We see the primitive hungers we live by and yet, by a curious feat of stoicism, fatalism, and lethargy, the passions of human nature are sceptically contained." Pritchett suggests that a clue to the Spanish temperament may be found in Spain's geography. If Spaniards have anything in common, it is not their nationality. "For the Spaniards are not Spaniards first, if they are Spaniards in the end. The peninsula is a piece of rocky geography. It is the subject of Spanish rhetoric, the occasion for their talk about Spanishness, for chauvinism and rebellion. . . ."

The easiest way to view Spain geographically is to think of it as a remote, isolated fort or castle. The Iberian Peninsula, containing Spain and Portugal, is surrounded by the Atlantic Ocean and the Mediterranean except for a strip of land less than 300 miles long which cuts it off from France. But this land separating it from the rest of Europe is the jagged range of the Pyrenees, which can be crossed by roads through only 10 passes. The narrow coastal plain all around most of the country is backed by ranges of mountains. The central plateau of Castile is divided by other mountain ranges. The contrasts in climate—from snow-capped peaks to lush, subtropical farmland—are enormous. Vegetation is similarly varied. For example, of the 10,000 varieties of wild flowers which are found in Europe, at least half are found only in Spain.

Spain can be divided into several mainland regions, and the differences which survive in all these regions are centuries old. Some of the differences, even in speech (particularly between Catalonia and the Basque Provinces), are perhaps greater than the differences which divide Spain itself from Portugal. It might therefore be profitable to take a tour of some of the major regions.

GALICIA is in the extreme northwest of Spain. Its climate is generally wet, much like that of Ireland. Most of the people are fishermen or farmers, and many of the peasant proprietors farm small strips of land belonging to a single owner. The soft gray land is poor, but the Galicians are a shrewd, thrifty and hardworking people. They speak a distinct dialect that is close to Portuguese. The great city of Galicia is Santiago de Compostela. Pilgrims from all over Europe know its magnificent cathedral, begun in 1078, which houses the shrine of Santiago or St. James. Another city, El Ferrol, was the birthplace of General Franco, who shares in full measure the proverbial Galician characteristics of prudence and caution.

Asturias might be called the cradle of Spain, for it was in this wild mountain territory that the Visigothic nobles and the remnants of their followers gathered after the Moorish conquests

had scooped up all the rest of Spain. The mountainous shrine at Covadonga is the place where Pelayo, the first Christian king of the *Reconquista*, defeated a Moorish army about 720 A.D. More recently the mountains of Asturias have produced large quantities of coal and iron. The miners of Asturias generally make themselves heard by opposing nearly all central government regimes. It was in Asturias in 1934, two years before the outbreak of the Spanish Civil War, that the miners acted out a curtain raiser to the war by holding out for almost two weeks against the right-wing government of the day—only to be crushed by the Foreign Legion and General Franco, who was already a prominent army officer.

LEON, one of the first of Spain's Christian kingdoms, produces wheat and cattle, and its province of Salamanca breeds fighting bulls. It is a conservative area, and its people have not shared very much in the industrial revolution. But the city of Salamanca, with its rich Roman, Gothic and Renaissance architecture and its university (founded about 1230 A.D.), was for centuries a meeting place of Europe's most learned men.

Old Castile is the heart of Spain, where the purest Spanish language (Castilian) is spoken. The region is the inspiration of the most characteristic Spanish traditions (notably the chivalry of El Cid and the deep faith of St. Theresa). For centuries the Castilian has been a particularly proud and unyielding breed of Spaniard. Old Castile is a big and in some places sparsely populated plateau hemmed in by mountains. Many of its tenant farmers are desperately poor and often neck-deep in debt.

The best-known cities of Old Castile are: Segovia, Avila, Burgos, Valladolid and Soria. Burgos, a solemn city with a magnificent Gothic cathedral, was the old capital of Castile before the reconquest of Toledo in 1085. Segovia, with its awe-inspiring Roman aqueduct, is a fascinating amalgam of Roman and Moorish and Christian cultures—the Alcázar (fortress-castle) and the stately Gothic cathedral are especially notable. Valladolid was at times, during the 14th and 15th Centuries, a favorite residence of the kings of Castile. Ferdinand and Isabella were married there in 1469, Philip II was born there in 1527 and Christopher Columbus died there in 1506. Valladolid was for many generations celebrated for its silversmiths—as well as for its pickpockets—but more recently for its importance as an industrial center.

NEW CASTILE forms the whole of the south section of the central plain of Spain. The province's most striking piece of architecture is the Escorial, a great, gray monastery-palace built by Philip II, who boasted that from his rooms there he was able to rule half the world with a couple of inches of paper. New Castile is centered on the great plain known as La Mancha, across whose wastes Don Quixote wandered with Sancho Panza in Cervantes' novel. Madrid, the first city, is the hub of most of the Franco regime's building program. The old part of Madrid has narrow, picturesque streets, but in general the city is a handsome open place of broad avenues. The climate, much maligned as being three months of winter and nine of summer hell, is actually excellent except in July and August. The government ministries, great banks and foreign embassies are in Madrid. General Franco lives in El Pardo, a former royal palace nine miles north.

Because Madrid was the court capital from the 16th Century on, its history is synonymous with that of Spain. The city became the acknowledged first city of the land after its heroic street mobs attacked the soldiers of Napoleon in 1808. The Puerta del Sol (an open plaza in front of the Ministry of the Interior) has long been the scene of riots and demonstrations which have often led to the fall of governments. The nearby cafés have been the setting for *tertulias* (discussion groups) that have sometimes bloomed into revolutionary parties. The second most important city in New Castile is Toledo, "the imperial city." It was the Old Visigothic capital, the capital of Spain off and on from the late 11th until the mid-16th Century and the religious capital of Spain since its reconquest from the Moors. Today it is the seat of the Primate or first archbishop of Spain. The city is now virtually a living museum, dominated by the paintings and the personality of El Greco, who lived there.

The region produces wheat and olives, grown on vast, rolling estates. The whole country has hardly changed in appearance since it took part, almost as a character, in *Don Quixote*. As in Old Castile, tenant farmers live in bleak poverty (although in both provinces many are now leaving the land for jobs in the cities).

Estremadura is the most backward region in Spain; the major portion of the area is either uncultivable sierra or large estates. The towns are poor, although Cáceres, Trujillo and Mérida are interesting to tourists. Mérida was once the Roman capital of Spain, and remnants remain of a theater, amphitheater, bridge and aqueduct. This region is part of today's news because of the ambitious Badajoz plan, which has tackled the job of regulating the upper waters of the Guadiana River to bring irrigation to the surrounding wasteland *(Chapter 6)*.

ANDALUSIA is the huge southern region divided from Castile by the Sierra Morena. Large areas of it are mountainous and uncultivable. The remainder is the land of *latifundios*—enormous estates on which landless laborers *(braceros)* scratch a bare living. The exception is in the valley of the Guadalquivir River running from Cordova to Seville where the subtropical climate permits the growing of figs and almonds, and the pinkish hills are covered with olive trees. The Andalusians are known for their easy charm, for grace rather than force and for a slightly condescending attitude toward the rest of Spain. One of the great towns is Seville, where Christian and Moorish architecture mingle: there is a Gothic cathedral, but the Giralda tower and the Alcázar are Moorish. Seville is also a center of industry, with distilleries, aircraft factories, chemical and textile plants. It was once the thriving port where the treasure-heavy ships sailed up the Guadalquivir

River from the New World. Cordova, once the Moorish capital, is now a tired city like so many in the south. In the middle of its great mosque, during the reign of Charles I (1516-1556), somebody was misguided enough to build a cathedral. Granada, the last Moorish outpost (conquered in 1492), is celebrated for the Alhambra *(Chapter 9)* and for the terraced Generalife Gardens.

Andalusia is the backdrop for many of the things often mistakenly regarded as typically Spanish—the flamenco and gypsy dancing, the picturesque donkey, the rose in the teeth and the strumming guitar. Chiefly, these concepts are popular because such 19th Century travelers as Washington Irving, Prosper Mérimée and Théophile Gautier perpetuated them.

The people of the Basque Provinces (including a part of Navarre) speak a language whose origin is obscure. Still heard outside the big cities, the Basque tongue is so difficult to learn that it is said the devil spent seven years learning it and at the end knew only three words. This language, not taught in the public schools, is reputed to be extremely useful in the smuggling trade. The foresters, sardine fishermen and peasants who live in these narrow green valleys, which are frequently watered by gray skies, are simple, uncompromising, religious folk. (St. Ignatius of Loyola was a Basque.) The origin of the Basques is one of history's puzzles, but they have clearly managed to preserve their own racial idiosyncrasies for many centuries. Possibly they are simply the survivors of the original Iberians. In their remote hills they have succeeded through long periods in resisting foreign conquest.

ARAGON is a harsh region surrounded by mountains and dominated by the great river Ebro and the city of Saragossa. The latter is the capital and a large industrial town of Roman origin. In the past the primitive, stubborn natives were known for their violence, and the local nobles retained power of life and death over their dependents until the 18th Century. (Goya was an Aragonese.)

Catalonia, which during the Middle Ages was a separate principality, has since that time been Spain's most active industrial and commercial area. The brilliant city of Barcelona is Mediterranean in character. Throughout the whole area, Catalan, a Romance language not taught in state schools, is widely spoken. During the late Middle Ages, Catalonia was the thriving focal point of an advanced culture, and its trading ships for a time rivaled the Italian vessels in the Mediterranean.

EARLY in the 20th Century, a revival of industry once more made Catalonia commercially important, and Barcelona's population doubled to more than a million. Meanwhile, the city's working class (many of whom had come from Andalusia to find work) went over in a body to anarchism. As a result, for the first 30 years of this century, Barcelona, the most prosperous city in Spain, was the scene of constant riots, disorder and bloodshed. During the Civil War, Barcelona played an essential role and was the Republican capital in late 1937. The rest of the province is a fertile area of small holdings and prosperous tenant farmers.

Valencia and Murcia are regions inhabited by small farmers, and much of the best land is already irrigated. Valencia, a great seaport on the Mediterranean, is a beautiful metropolis noted for its graceful medieval and Renaissance architecture, and surrounded by fertile land so tempting that its inhabitants call it "a piece of heaven on earth."

Whether in its geography or in the temperament of its people, Spain makes its dramatic contrasts felt. The ground the Spanish rest their lives on, says V. S. Pritchett, is "something smaller than Spain. They are rooted in their region, even nowadays. . . . They are Basques, Catalans, Galicians, Castilians, Andalusians, Valencians, Murcians, and so on, before they are Spaniards; and before they are men of these regions they are men of some town or village; and in that place, small or large, they think perfection lies. . . ."

A padre from Castile and his dour sacristan confer on a sidewalk in Seville. They have journeyed together to attend Seville's Holy Week.

A Colorful and Contradictory People

Life in Spain gives off a note which, like Spanish guitar music, is both sweet and deeply melancholy. The Spanish are traditionally austere and ascetic, and yet they often can be seen to relax with unselfconscious grace. They take joy in the bloody spectacle of the bull ring, but they are gentle and kindly to foreign visitors. Absorbed in the mysteries of their religion, they live always with the consciousness of death— and respond by being sharply, explosively alive.

TRADITIONS dear to the tourist and Spaniard alike are the exotic rhythm of flamenco and the gaiety of fiesta-time

A FLAMENCO DANCER in the traditional long flounced skirt of the gypsy performer *(left)* twirls in staccato steps. Her body movements and the accompanying music are oriental in character. Like many other aspects of life in the south of Spain, where flamenco had its origin, this dance is believed to stem from Moorish influence.

THE SEVILLE FAIR brings out elegant riders wearing Andalusian costume to parade through gaily decorated streets —the men in close-fitting jackets and flat hats, their ladies in ruffled dresses seated behind. Most renowned of Spanish festivals, the *feria* lasts for six days following Holy Week, and features bullfights every afternoon.

BULLFIGHTING stirs the Spaniard's

love of grace, skill and danger

STAMPEDING BULLS pursue a crowd of young men into the arena in Pamplona. This frenzied prelude to the bullfight gives the men a chance to exhibit daring.

BOLD MATADOR in a gold-encrusted "suit of lights," Jaime Ostos pivots as the bull thunders by and hooks the red muleta with its horns. The most valued matadors are those who stand closest to the path of the horns and make "passes" with cape and muleta smoothly. Barbed sticks, *banderillas*, protrude from the bull's shoulders.

VIVID WITH LIFE, the well-worn byways of an ancient

town resound with the cries of children and the

laughter of adults unbowed by long years of toil and hardship

FENCING in mock combat, a group of small boys re-enact the battles of El Cid and the Moors among the ruins of a castle in the Mediterranean town of Peñíscola.

SCRUBBING the family wash, women of Peñíscola gather at an outdoor trough near the castle. They beat the clothes to get them clean and avoid using valuable soap.

CONVIVIALITY is
the order of the day
as men gather after work
to talk and play cards

A HEARTY JOKE is shared by card players sitting in a sunny café in Peñíscola. Joining in is one of the two Civil Guards assigned to patrol the Peñíscola waterfront. The Guardia Civil, which enforces laws imposed by the central government in Madrid, is despised by many Spaniards for whom the uniformed troopers evoke bitter memories of the Civil War. But over the years the guard has become a fixture of the rural scene, and individual guardsmen often are accepted members of local communities.

2

Early

Lessons

in Violence

SPANISH history differs strikingly from that of other leading European countries. Many western nations can boast a continuous if sometimes irregular improvement in standard of living and social justice. But no such comfortable generalization is possible about Spain. Roman Spain did more to improve communications and so tie the people of Spain together than did most later generations, and more middle-class Spaniards participated in their government in the 13th Century than do today.

During the 16th Century, Spain was the greatest nation on earth. Its intrepid little ships continually sailed west in the still sketchily charted Ocean Sea, and its vast territorial possessions eventually included all of South and Central America except Brazil, most of the southwest of the present United States, and large parts of Italy and the Low Countries. In addition, it enjoyed huge political power in Europe as the temporal sword of the Roman Catholic Church.

From the Middle Ages up to the present, the Church in Spain has played a special role: the history of medieval Spain might be regarded as a long religious-military crusade against Moslem control. In the 16th Century, the Spanish Church was the main instrument of national unity, and to a considerable degree the greatness

25

of Spain at that time derived from the greatness of the Church. In the ensuing centuries, the Church has tried to maintain its role as arbiter of the nation's cultural life, and many of Spain's political troubles have been inseparable from its religious troubles.

Despite Spain's past national greatness, the country's sense of national consciousness has evolved with great difficulty. Indeed, the history of Spain can be viewed as a perpetual see-saw between centralism and regionalism. Since the mid-18th Century, the advanced areas of Spain have been on the geographical edges (Barcelona, the Basque Provinces) and hence have always resisted control by the conservative and backward central regions. Many of the outer, prosperous regions have had autonomous aspirations and, in times of political turbulence, brief experience of independence. The working class has at times also rejected the idea that the nation was the most compelling force for holding its loyalties. As a result, both regional and class hatreds, as well as religious and ideological disputes, have plagued modern Spain. All these factors culminated in modern times in a tragic confession of national breakdown: the 1936-1939 Civil War.

S PAIN'S leading characteristics might suggest a nation that is politically unique and therefore lost to the general stream of European civilization. The fact is that Spain has been closely linked with other nations throughout its history. Sometimes the link was toward the Moslem world, sometimes toward the countries beyond the Pyrenees and sometimes toward the American continent. In most Spanish civil wars, there have been appeals to other countries for help. The current regime of General Franco, nationalist and isolationist though it is, was befriended in the United Nations by General Perón of Argentina, and in the 1950s it received economic aid, because of cold war expediency, from the United States. Military aid from Germany and Italy was of critical importance in establishing the regime. Spaniards, who understandably seek to convert their

proud isolationism into political ideology, make a sentimental ideal of the survival in Spain of certain aspects of preindustrial European society—including a sense of personal dignity, a lack of self-concern and a willingness to undertake violence. Much of Spanish history, in fact, reflects the country's ambivalent feeling of being emotionally attracted to, or repelled by, the general stream of European civilization.

B EFORE it could attain any sort of unity as a nation, the Spanish peninsula was for many centuries a battleground of invasion and resistance. Among the invaders, the Romans and the Moslems (the Spaniards called them Moors) probably left the deepest imprint on Spanish life and customs. But their mark was made upon a people who were already mixed. In the mists of prehistory, Cro-Magnon man left his testament in the caves of Altamira: red-and-black paintings of bison, horses, boar and deer that have been called "the Sistine Chapel of prehistoric art." During a later era, the inhabitants of the peninsula are believed to have exported copper and silver to other Mediterranean lands.

The Iberians, a people thought to be of North African stock, started to settle around 3000 B.C. in the south and east of the peninsula to which they eventually gave their name. Their culture was absorbed by the Romans at about the time of Christ. Early Roman writers describe the Iberians as dark, wiry men with prominent cheekbones who were "morally noble, hospitable and religious, though arrogant and lazy." After 1000 B.C., the Celts poured down through the Pyrenees in successive waves to dominate the northern regions of present-day Spain.

The inhabitants of the Iberian peninsula often felt the influence of more advanced trading peoples of the eastern Mediterranean. First came the Phoenicians in the Ninth Century B.C., bringing with them the idea of commerce, the technique of writing, the use of gold and silver jewelry, and a fairly well-developed system of mining. Their most important settlement—Gadir, the modern Cádiz—had a magnificent temple to Baal.

The Greeks, who had traded with the Iberian Peninsula since the Seventh Century B.C., eventually came to set up trading colonies. Their main trading post was at Ampurias (from the Greek word for market place) in Catalonia, and they introduced the vine and the olive to Spain.

In the Sixth Century, the Phoenician settlers in Gadir asked Carthage, a Phoenician colony in North Africa, for assistance in repulsing an attack by native tribes, and the Carthaginians came and stayed on. They gave the region a name: Span or Spania, meaning "land of rabbits." At first the Carthaginians' ambitions were restricted to commerce and exploitation of Spain's rich silver mines, but rivalry with Rome soon spurred them to widen their control of the peninsula. In the course of this attempt, a Carthaginian leader named Hannibal, who was the greatest of the Barcas (a distinguished military family that gave its name to Barcelona), attacked Saguntum, a city under the protection of Carthage's old enemy, Rome. Then came the first of several European conflicts in which Spain was both battleground and prize: the Second Punic War (218-201 B.C.), whose consequence was the final victory of Rome and the beginning of Roman dominance of Spain.

It took the Romans more than two centuries to subdue the whole peninsula. The struggle was notable for the heroism of the ex-shepherd Viriatus, who united his fellow tribesmen and temporarily reconquered a great deal of western and central Spain from the Romans. The conflict was also memorable because of the legendary two-decade defense of the city of Numantia. In this protracted siege, the Numantians fought until they were all killed in battle or had committed suicide. Only rubble was left of the city.

FINALLY achieving mastery over the peninsula in the First Century A.D., the Romans built a state authority more efficient and unquestioned than many that have followed. Their greatest contributions were in law and administration. Efficient Roman rule brought peace, and Roman law emphasized the rights of the individual rather than his obligations to family

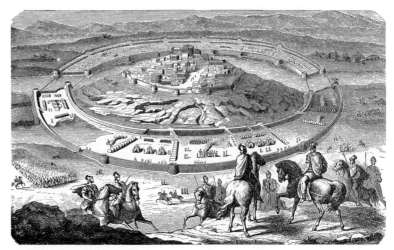

BESIEGED BY THE ROMANS, the fortified settlement of Numantia fell to the invaders in 133 B.C. Its capture forecast the final Roman subjugation of the peninsula.

and tribe. Unification was attempted through a deliberate policy of breaking up the tribes or changing their dwellings. Latin became the official language. The people of Spain were gradually allowed to become full Roman citizens. Towns were developed as centers of governmental authority as well as of trade.

The prosperity of Roman Spain may sometimes have been exaggerated, but there can be no question that commerce flourished—especially in olive oil, wheat, wax, wine, pepper and honey. Magnificent roads and bridges, some still in use today, facilitated communication among the peoples. The Roman cities were large, and they were both culturally and economically active. Many of the leading men of action and letters in the Roman Empire (notably Trajan, Hadrian, Marcus Aurelius, Theodosius, Seneca, Quintilian and Martial) came from Spain—though probably most were of Roman rather than native Spanish origin. On the peninsula, as elsewhere in Europe, the three long centuries of Roman peace—even when broken by civil wars for power inside the empire—were nostalgically recalled through many troubled generations that followed.

The Germanic invasion of Spain began in 409, with the arrival of the Suevi, the Alans and the Vandals, who destroyed a great deal in

Roman Spain, as elsewhere in Europe. They were followed in 411 by the Visigoths, who had already sacked Rome. The Visigoths were not only partially Romanized but had accepted, by the Third Century, the Arian version of Christianity. Ultimately successful in overwhelming the other Germanic invaders, the Visigoths established themselves as rulers of the entire Iberian Peninsula. Throughout the next two and a half centuries (circa 456-711) they ruled from the new capital of Toledo, located in the central plateau area of Spain that has continued to be politically prominent.

Visigoths and Hispano-Romans lived side by side for a time, following their own laws and different versions of Christianity. However, Visigothic rule was never more than that of a minority attempting to maintain itself over a more sophisticated Romanized majority, and the Visigoths gradually accepted Roman customs and habits. In 587 King Reccared and many of the Visigoths abandoned Arian Christianity for Roman Catholicism. In the mid-Seventh Century, the Gothic and Roman laws were recast into a single code—the Liber Judicorum—and laws which hampered the development of peaceful relations between the two peoples were abolished. But complete fusion was not achieved. Through the centuries of Visigothic rule, the Jews, who had come to Spain in considerable numbers, became increasingly oppressed.

UNLIKE the Roman rulers, the Visigoths preferred rural to urban life. They were easily distinguished from the Hispano-Romans because they wore their hair long; cutting off a Visigoth's hair incapacitated him for public office, especially for kingship. The games and arena fights of the Roman period died out and were replaced by bullfights. There are typical Visigothic churches in Spain today, notably the Church of San Juan de Baños in Palencia.

The question of succession to the throne troubled much of the Visigothic era in Spain. The succession laws made it possible for any noble to be elected, and each king who won by strength tried to arrange that his sons should succeed. These conflicts over the kingship eventually led to disaster. In 710, Achila, the king's son, had assumed the throne without election. He was deposed by a candidate selected by the nobility. Achila's supporters appealed for help to the Moors (the Moslem inhabitants of Morocco). As new converts to Islam, the Moors were afire with religious zeal. They crossed over into Spain, defeated the king and then proceeded to sweep Achila and his supporters aside. Within seven years the Moors had conquered the whole peninsula except for a few outposts in the northern mountains.

MOORISH Spain eventually became the artistic and commercial center of the entire Mediterranean area. Life in Spain felt the impact of a new culture and luxury that had strong eastern and Greek influences. In the Ninth and 10th Centuries, Cordova was a city of 113,000 houses, 700 mosques and 300 public baths. Its streets were paved, and water was piped to its residents. The Sultan's library contained 400,000 volumes, and the University of Cordova had schools of medicine, mathematics, poetry, astronomy and theology.

Among the architectural achievements of the Moors were the solution of the problem of balancing huge weights on slight supports and the intercrossing of arches and the interlaced moldings of a dome. From this period, "arabesque" decoration (plaques of marble or plaster carved in geometrical or floral designs) is the most outstanding artistic legacy.

In agriculture the Moors introduced new crops (notably figs, dates, rice, cane and cotton) and extended irrigation. The Moors in Spain had the largest merchant marine in the Mediterranean, and they expanded the mining, stock raising, and wool and silk industries.

Politically and socially the Moslems appeared to be so sure of themselves that they showed great tolerance toward their subjects who were of both Visigothic and Hispano-Roman origin. Christian rites were permitted, and there were even some Christian holidays (such as St. John's Day) which were observed by Moslems and

Christians together. In the time of the great General Almansor (who himself was married to a Christian princess), Moslem troops—among whom were many Christian mercenaries—observed Sunday as a holiday. In at least one instance, Moslems and Christians used different sections of the same building for worship, one part serving as a mosque, another as a church. Mixed marriages were common.

For more than three centuries the greater part of Spain remained under Moslem rule, but during all these years descendants of Visigoths and Hispano-Romans were united at least in a desire for reconquest—*Reconquista*. As early as 718 A.D., a Visigoth noble named Pelayo led the remnants of the Christian armies that had gathered in the mountains of Asturias into victorious battle against the Moslems. The *Reconquista* had begun. It did not end until Granada was conquered at the close of the Middle Ages, in 1492.

PELAYO'S successors, over a couple of centuries, extended their Asturian realm to include León and Castile. They also gained a tenuous hold on Galicia and Navarre. This nascent unity of the Christian domains disintegrated some decades later when Castile and Navarre again splintered off into independent kingdoms.

Until the 11th Century the *Reconquista* was a haphazard affair, motivated largely by the desire of nobles and churchmen to regain their lost estates. But early in the 11th Century the Moslem empire fell apart into squabbling independent units. With the Moslems weakened by division, the Christians, inspired by the crusading spirit then prevalent in Europe, gradually overcame their own internal disorder and started making decisive gains. In 1085 Alfonso VI of León and Castile conquered Toledo. This was the most signal victory of the *Reconquista* to date.

At first the Christian conquerors treated the defeated Moslems with a tolerance which almost matched that of the Moslems to Christians: in Toledo, as in other conquered areas, the national and religious customs of four separate groups were guaranteed. But throughout the *Reconquista* it was the policy of the Christian monarchs of the north to attempt to colonize the usually barren, unpopulated land they conquered. Hence the cities which grew up around Castile's forts or castles (the numbers of which gave the kingdom its name) were composed to a great extent of northern colonists—Basques and Navarrese.

The *Reconquista* had, of course, its representative hero about whom many legends grew up. He was El Cid Campeador (The Warrior Lord)—Rodrigo Díaz, a brilliant, chivalrous and self-seeking warrior. In the time of El Cid, the self-made man was a popular hero in Castile, and ownership of a horse was a necessary mark of prestige. El Cid was thus the perfect *caballero*—a gentleman on horseback. He married the niece of King Alfonso VI but offended that monarch by setting out on his own to attack the Moorish kingdom of Toledo, over which Alfonso had established a protectorate. El Cid was, therefore, exiled from Castile and went to fight in the service of the Moors. He eventually conquered Valencia for himself and lived there as ruler until he died in 1099.

His career was curiously ambiguous for a Christian hero, but it illustrates the character of these century-long conflicts: war between Christian and Moslem was not continuous, only seasonal. In time of peace there were close relations between the two sides. Various Moorish kings often sought help from Christians to fight their Moslem rivals.

THE greatest series of conquests against the Moslems took place in the 13th Century. The turning point was the Battle of Navas de Tolosa, when the Moslems were driven south of the Sierra Morena; in 1236 King Ferdinand III of León and Castile (later canonized as St. Ferdinand) captured Cordova, and 12 years later he took Seville. King Jaime of Aragon took the Balearic Islands and later Valencia. This reduced Moslem holdings to the kingdom of Granada and some of the small areas west of Seville. The Christians were able to consolidate their victory because the Castilian kings had succeeded in permanently uniting their own territory with that of León, Galicia and Asturias, while the enlarged kingdom of Aragon had merged in 1137 with Catalonia. These two kingdoms—Castile and Aragon— mutually agreed on boundaries for their respective conquests of Moslem territory. On the west coast, Portugal began to develop into a separate kingdom.

The general shape of a nation was emerging. Although the rise of two strong Christian monarchies in Spain in the 13th Century was to have a marked effect on later history, it did not lead to a quick final victory over the Moslems, as might have been expected. Ferdinand of Castile was followed for the next two centuries by a series of rather inadequate kings who were preoccupied with dynastic struggles and disputes with the nobility. At the same time, the kings of Aragon embarked on a series of successful Mediterranean adventures. In the end, the Aragonese kings gathered to themselves a maritime empire that included not only the Balearic Islands but southern Italy, Sicily and Sardinia as well.

OUTSIDE the court life of medieval Spain, a quite different society existed. In each community, individuals and groups were struggling to gain various kinds of rights. By about 1200, despite the wide local power possessed by nobles, the serfs of León and Castile had succeeded in forcing their lords to define the work they had to perform and had secured the abolition of the custom of selling serfs along with land. In Aragon no such exceptions to a lord's rights were made: as late as the early 18th Century, the nobles of Aragon had complete powers of life and death over their serfs.

The growth of towns during the *Reconquista* brought a democratic habit founded on the idea of the assembly of the whole community. This habit had a national consequence in the growth of *cortes* (literally, courts), or parliaments. At these courts, the popular element, alongside the nobles and clergy, was represented as advisers to the king. This precocious parliamentary system, with popular representation, was born in León before the end of the 12th Century and functioned surprisingly well in the kingdoms of all of Christian Spain by the 13th Century. The *cortes* voted on taxes, approved expenditures requested by the king, voiced grievances and made petitions to the crown for new laws or revision of old laws. Though the effective power of these early parliaments was limited, few people in Europe at that time played such an important role in their own government as did the Spaniards.

THE desire to create a unified kingdom never seems to have been a strong motive in the *Reconquista,* nor was it a motive for the aggrandizement of Christian kings. The one force that did help bring all Spain together was the Roman Catholic Church. All Christians could unite on the need for driving out the infidels. During the *Reconquista*, the Church gathered vast estates throughout Spain, and the clergy became exempt from both taxation and ordinary law. The Romanesque and Gothic churches that still stand are the permanent artistic record of this age of religion.

At the end of the 15th Century, four events shaped the destiny of the emerging nation:

In 1469, Ferdinand, the heir of Aragon, married Isabella, the Queen Regnant of Castile, thus preparing the way for the union of the crowns of the two important territories and the creation of the Spain of modern boundaries.

The same two monarchs finally conquered the last Moslem outpost in Granada in 1492. The *Reconquista* was thus complete.

Also in 1492, Christopher Columbus, with the blessing of Ferdinand and Isabella, set out on the epoch-making voyage that resulted in the discovery of the New World and the far-flung overseas Spanish Empire.

Finally, Ferdinand and Isabella jointly broke the power of the nobility and, by a number of administrative reforms, prepared the way for a modern nation-state.

A stately Roman aqueduct, nearly 2,000 years old, throws shadows on a street in Segovia. It still supplies the city with water.

Echoing a Turbulent and Glorious Past

The face of Spain bears the marks of a long, varied and often tragic history. There are constant reminders of Roman conquest and Roman civilization. Magnificent castles and mosques testify to the lengthy occupation by the Moors.

Massive palaces and lofty cathedrals reflect the ambition of Spain's monarchs during their centuries of power. It seems not surprising that the Spanish people, living among so many relics, have often tended to cling to old ways.

31

QUIET GARDENS with delicate fountains *(opposite)* grace the courtyards of the Alhambra. The columns and festooned arches are characteristic of ornate Moorish design.

ROSE-COLORED STRUCTURES of the Alhambra stand on a hill in Granada. A seat of Moorish kings, it was begun in the 13th Century. Christian forces captured it in 1492.

GAUNT WINDMILL stands against the horizon of La Mancha. Cervantes' Don Quixote, who was from La Mancha, engaged such windmills in demented combat.

WALLED CITY of Avila was founded by the Romans and several times changed hands in the long wars between Christians and Moors. The walls were rebuilt in 1090 by Alfonso VI of León and Castile, who ringed the town with 88 towers. Their battlements still command a strategic passage through the mountains of central Spain.

3

The Era
of
Greatness

MANY Spaniards still think of Isabella as their greatest ruler—and with very good reason. During her reign (1474-1504), Spain moved into *el siglo de oro* (the golden century) —an era of power and leadership in world affairs that it has never had since. Spain's period as the leading nation of the world began with two events successfully launched in 1492 by Ferdinand of Aragon and Isabella of Castile: the discovery of the New World and the final conquest of the Moors. The time of greatness continued through the reign of Isabella's grandson, Charles I. The great days had begun to fade by 1588, when Philip II, Isabella's great-grandson, suffered the crushing humiliation of losing Spain's powerful Armada to the English queen, Elizabeth.

In retrospect, it is easy to see why Spain's power, dominant in European affairs for so long, dwindled so inexorably. Instead of concentrating on developing its own resources and the colonies it had gained in America, Spain made the mistake of insisting on being the strongest and most influential country in Europe—and thereby overreached itself. Spain had a better start than England at being Europe's dominant nation, but much of its best resources of manpower were drained off by the

37

The Era of Greatness

American colonies, and its gold from the New World was squandered in fruitless wars and political intrigues in Italy, Germany, France and the Low Countries.

The great century of Spanish predominance was also one of religious zeal and intolerance. Not only did Spain fight to maintain the Catholic faith against the inroads of Protestantism and other heresies, but the Spanish state itself was rent by tension between Christians and converts. Spanish missionaries unquestionably did work of lasting importance in the New World, but in Spain itself Ferdinand and Isabella, in their zeal to convert or get rid of Moors and Jews and uproot heresy in general, initiated policies that led to the terrors and tortures of the Spanish Inquisition.

The discovery of America by Christopher Columbus has made the names of Ferdinand and Isabella, the "Catholic Sovereigns," more or less familiar to every schoolboy. It was with royal backing that the Genoese map maker-sailor set out from Palos on August 3, 1492, to search for a western route to Cathay. Columbus and his three little vessels, *Niña, Pinta* and *Santa María,* sailed due west after pausing briefly at the Canary Islands. Fortunately, they struck favorable trade winds. It was one of the most remarkable voyages in the history of mankind, and yet the men who made it lived as ordinary seamen did in the Middle Ages. Columbus, the Admiral, saw to it that there were formal religious services several times a day aboard the three ships, with many a *gracias a Dios* for good weather. The "victualling," as Columbus called it in a letter to his sovereigns, consisted of a sort of hardtack, plus "wine,

FERDINAND AND ISABELLA united Spain by their marriage in 1469 and began the country's epoch of power.

salt meat, oil, vinegar, cheese, chickpeas, lentils, beans, salt fish and fishing tackle, honey, rice, almonds and raisins."

On October 8, Columbus noted in his Journal: "Thanks be to God the air is soft as in April in Seville, and it's a pleasure to be in it, so fragrant it is." During all of the following night, the seamen heard birds flying southwestward. On October 10, when land was less than 200 miles away, discontent among the men over the long, boring voyage almost flared into mutiny, but the Admiral sailed on. Then, early on the morning of October 12, the lookout on *Pinta* saw something like a white sand cliff gleaming in the moonlight. *"Tierra! Tierra!"* he shouted—and indeed, land it was: the coral island of San Salvador in the Bahamas.

On this first voyage Columbus also touched at Cuba and at Hispaniola. He returned to Spain on March 15, 1493, to the admiration and gratitude of the court and the excited interest of all Europe.

On his second voyage (1493-1496), Columbus set out with 17 ships and some 1,200 to 1,500 men, including sailors, artisans, colonists, officials and priests. They carried seeds, domestic animals and farm implements, hoping to found a mining-agricultural colony and to transplant Spanish life to the New World. "No European nation," says historian Samuel Eliot Morison, "had ever undertaken an overseas colonizing expedition on anything approaching this scale."

On this voyage Columbus discovered most of the Lesser Antilles and Puerto Rico; on his third trip (1498-1500), he sailed along the Venezuelan coast; on his fourth (1502-1504), he explored from Honduras to Panama. Columbus always believed that he had found a western route to the Orient. He thought that the islands which are still called the West Indies were part of the Malay Archipelago.

With exploration the order of the day, there were other expeditions during which all of Central and South America (except Brazil) and large areas of what is now the southern United States were explored and linked to Spain as colonies. (Brazil was allotted to Portugal as a result of the Treaty of Tordesillas of 1494.)

IT was a time of great Spanish heroes. Hernán Cortés launched his conquest of Mexico with 500 men, and Francisco Pizarro took Peru with less than 200. Ferdinand Magellan sailed out of a Spanish port in 1519. He died in the Philippines, but one of his captains, a Basque named Juan Sebastián del Cano, completed the first journey around the world. Shiploads of gold and silver began to be brought back from the new colonies. The *conquistadores* were avid for new discoveries and dedicated to the conversion of the natives of the new lands. Meanwhile, King Ferdinand prodded Spain into an attempt to take the lead in European affairs. In the long run, this effort frittered away many of Spain's colonial gains made by Spain's *conquistadores*. But Ferdinand wrested a few provinces from France, and in 1504, thanks to the military genius of Gonzalo Fernández de Córdoba—El Gran Capitán—Ferdinand succeeded in getting Naples under his control.

The daughter of Ferdinand and Isabella, Juana "La Loca" (The Crazy), was too mentally unstable to take the throne. Her son, Charles I, began his kingship blessed with well-to-do grandparents. His mother's parents passed on to him the rule of Castile, Aragon, Navarre, Roussillon and Cerdagne astride the Pyrenees, Sardinia, Sicily and Naples, as well as domains in Africa and America. His father, Philip the Handsome, was the son of the Hapsburg Holy Roman Emperor Maximilian I and of Mary of Burgundy. Through his paternal grandmother, Charles inherited the territories of the House of Burgundy (Flanders and Artois in northern France, Franche-Comté and Charolais in the east, Luxembourg and the Low Countries); and through his grandfather (Maximilian) he held domains in central Europe and a claim to the title of Holy Roman Emperor. When Emperor Maximilian I died in 1519, Charles, through bribery, got himself elected Holy Roman Emperor. His title as emperor was Charles V; as king of Spain, Charles I.

His character was one of the most curious in European history. Cautious, conscientious, vacillating but courageous, he had the bad luck of facing the full blast of the Reformation movement in his German dominions. During most of his reign, he was busy with revolts inside Spain and with foreign wars to hold or enlarge his vast, far-flung European territories. He spent much of his time outside Spain, but he abdicated to die in a monastery at Yuste, leaving his Spanish, Italian and Low Country dominions and some special instruction in kingship to his son, Philip II. He arranged to have his brother Ferdinand made Holy Roman Emperor. He left behind a Spain that was deeply suspicious of the religious sincerity of forcibly converted Jews and Moslems.

The reforms made within the Spanish Church were enough to prevent Protestantism from making much headway, although a few intellectuals were attracted by the new ideas. But any suspected heresy or lapses by "new" Christians were firmly dealt with by the Inquisition.

THE Inquisition was a system set up to rout out and punish heresy. In its excessive zeal to grasp more and more power, it was not generally popular with Spaniards. But it was so pampered and protected by the kings that its decisions tended to become final, with no appeal or recourse allowed. The first *auto de fe* (act of faith) was held in 1481, and 16 people were burned to death. Even some books that had been approved by Rome appeared on the Inquisition's Index of forbidden works. So many suspected heretics were arrested and tried that people of outstanding purity of faith were sometimes caught in the Inquisition's net—among them Theresa of Jesus, who was later canonized. In an era when a main preoccupation of Spaniards was the salvation of their souls, the Inquisition was correctly regarded by the kings as a powerful spur to religious unity and thus to national solidarity.

The second important force in the Spanish Counter Reformation was the Jesuit order (the Company of Jesus). Founded by a Spaniard, Ignatius of Loyola (1491-1556), it grew in political importance both in Spain and in the rest of the world. As a young man, Ignatius led the happy-go-lucky life of a soldier. Wounded by the French in 1521 during the defense of Pamplona, he spent a long convalescence reading devotional books and resolved to consecrate his life to religious work. In preparation, he studied at the Universities of Barcelona, Alcalá de Henares, Salamanca and Paris. Arrested by agents of the Inquisition while still a student, he was let off with a warning to stop wearing sackcloth and preaching in the streets.

CHARLES I inherited vast domains, ruling over Spain, the Low Countries and a large part of the rest of Europe.

Ignatius' new order was organized along strict military lines, with the members vowing unquestioning obedience to the Pope. Education was chosen as their chief missionary instrument.

The Jesuits were at first unpopular with many Spaniards, both clerical and secular, but late in his life Philip II finally realized that the new order, which had been formally approved by the Pope in 1540, was an effective force for religious unification of his dominions and as such furthered his dream of a centralized nation. Some Jesuits eventually won the respect of the Spanish people by becoming renowned throughout Europe as the most learned men of their time. They were also highly effective missionaries in the New World. Through the

centuries the militantly Christian order, usually working through the rich and powerful, has been a social force to be reckoned with in almost all Spanish-speaking lands.

Throughout the era of greatness, members of the Spanish court dressed extravagantly and enjoyed extravagant pastimes. Kings and noblemen turned toreador in the bull ring, and spent prodigious amounts on horses and helpers. Both men and women wore bright-colored clothing, with ruffs, puffs, ribbons and rings, fancy laces, openwork bodices, pretentious purses, pouches and other accessories which must have been thought ornamental since they were only barely useful. Even deeply religious and usually austere Isabella liked to appear on formal occasions lavishly gowned and sparkling with jewels. One 16th Century visitor from Italy expressed the thought that the Spaniard is prodigal on holidays, and then lives leanly for the rest of the year, because his occasional extravagances demand long periods of drab economy.

King Philip II, despite his Austrian blood and the disasters that plagued his reign, typifies Spain at its high point. Philip was a small, excessively tidy man with a melancholy look in his pale blue eyes and with his yellow hair and beard cut short. He preferred to dress in plain black velvet without the ribbons, laces and jewels that were the fashion of the day. His physical monument is the vast, austere, half-monastery, half-palace at Escorial, near Madrid. From gloomy cell-like quarters there, he directed his empire, personally intervening in all administrative questions. He enjoyed all the details of administration—conferring with his ministers, diplomats and secret agents from all over Europe, dictating letters and annotating the margins, inventing codes and filing systems. The only thing about administration that he hated was making up his mind. He therefore vacillated and took too long at the tasks of government, but he had a tenacious desire to inflate, develop and centralize the monarchy and to stamp out Protestantism. Under such able generals as the Duke of Alba, the Spanish army came to be feared throughout Europe. A major development of Philip's reign was his assumption of the crown of Portugal, which he gathered to his other dominions in 1581. Portugal remained under Spanish rule for the next 60 years.

In spite of Philip II's undoubted position at the summit of Spain's golden century, his reign marks the start of the country's long decline. A rebellion in the Low Countries not only wasted vast quantities of Spanish treasure and manpower, but gave the Netherlands its independence. The armies sent to France to fight with the Catholics in the religious wars against the Huguenots were further drains.

PHILIP II presided over a Spain that was supreme, but his actions led to the beginning of the country's decline.

From the moment in 1558 when Protestant Elizabeth succeeded Catholic Mary on the throne of England, there was a constant threat of open warfare between England and Spain. Philip knew that a Protestant on the English throne was a serious blow to his hopes for a Catholic Europe. Undeclared war was already raging in the Caribbean, where English pirates (notably Francis Drake, who was later knighted for his unofficial services to his queen) were firing on Spanish ships and sacking Spanish settlements. But Philip knew that an attack on the island stronghold of England would cost a staggering amount of money, so he postponed a formal declaration of war for nearly 30 years.

Finally making up his mind, he launched his *Armada Invencible* against the English in 1588.

Although the fleet seemed as invincible as its name—it consisted of 131 ships with more than 25,000 sailors, soldiers and officers—the entire project was bungled from beginning to end. Philip insisted on personally directing, from the Escorial, every move the fleet made, putting the expedition in nominal charge of the Duke of Medina Sidonia, who had an impeccable family background but knew nothing whatever about seamanship. The description of the fleet given by the American historian J. L. Motley suggests that the Armada may have been more handsome than it was efficient:

"The galleons were huge, round-stemmed clumsy vessels . . . built up at stem and stern, like castles. The galeasses . . . were rowed each by 300 galley-slaves. They consisted of an enormous towering fortress at the stern, a castellated structure almost equally massive in front, with seats for the rowers amidships. At stem and stern and between each of the slaves' benches were heavy cannon. These galeasses were floating edifices, very wonderful to contemplate. They were gorgeously decorated. . . . To take part in an ostentatious pageant, nothing could be better devised. To fulfill the great objects of a war vessel —to sail and to fight—they were the worst machines ever launched upon the ocean. . . . All the ships of the fleet—galeasses, galleys, galleons, and hulks—were so encumbered with top-hamper, so overweighted in proportion to their draught of water, that they could bear but little canvas, even with smooth seas and light and favorable winds."

One of the English captains of the fleet that engaged the Armada at Plymouth in July 1588 was Sir Francis Drake. Firing at long range with superior fire power, the English forced the

41

Spaniards up the Channel and damaged them in three engagements. At Calais they sent fire ships among the Spanish and defeated them at close range. The Spaniards tried to retreat by sailing up around Scotland and down the west coast of Ireland, but nothing went right. They ran into heavy storms, their provisions gave out and many were killed or captured by the Irish. Only 65 ships and some 10,000 men finally limped back to Spain.

The defeat of the Armada was not quite the end of Spain's era of greatness, but it was a humiliating forerunner of grayer days to come. Spain was not to recover from the many grave mistakes made by the kings of the golden century. Yet their imprint remains in the Americas. Today, in most of the New World south of the United States, Spanish is still the dominant language, and Catholicism is the dominant religion.

Before Philip died in 1598, he said of his son, who later became Philip III: "God, who has given me so many kingdoms, has denied me a son capable of ruling them." During the 17th Century reigns of Philip III, Philip IV and Charles II, each one weaker than his predecessor, Spain lost its front rank position in European affairs. Costly wars continued in France, Germany and the Low Countries. Jamaica, lost to England, was the first of many colonies in America to slip from Spain's control.

BY the end of the 16th Century, the fledgling economic revival brought on by American trade was petering out. Spain's military decline was matched by an economic collapse. The vast imports of gold and silver from the New World caused a catastrophic rise in prices and did not come in fast enough to pay for the costly military ventures all over Europe.

By expelling the Jews, the Spanish kings lost many of the people who formed the professional structure of the nation. As Américo Castro, the modern Spanish historian, put it, "the Christian knew little of the art of producing and conveying wealth, and he looked with surprised and hostile eyes upon the industry of the Jews and Moors" and at their "diligence in manual labor." There had been considerable economic development since the reign of the Catholic Sovereigns, particularly in wool and other textiles, but the Spanish people began to get the idea that the hard work involved in manual labor was somehow ignoble.

CONCURRENT with the economic decline came a decline in the spirit of such proto-democratic institutions as existed in Spain. The *cortes* of Castile, the councils of nobles, churchmen and burghers which since the 13th Century had been advising the crown, were convoked 44 times between 1517 and 1665, but there was no public interest. The kings gained increasing control over the deputies, and representatives often sold their seats to others. In 1665 a royal decree transferred to Castile's town councils the right to grant taxes, and for the next half century the *cortes* were not called at all. The *cortes* of other regions continued to meet, but their power was negligible.

Most of the 16th Century and the first half of the 17th was nonetheless the highest point in Spanish art and literature. This subject is discussed in Chapter 9; but in making any judgment of this period, note should be taken of the fact that Spain's military and economic losses were balanced by the work of such artists as El Greco, Ribera, Zurbarán, Velázquez and Murillo among painters and by the writings of such men as St. John of the Cross, Cervantes, Lope de Vega and Calderón.

The decline of Spain continued throughout the 17th Century, although the other nations of Europe hardly realized that it was going on. The defeat of Spanish troops by France at Rocroi in 1643 was the military turning point and indicated how far beneath the high standards of Alba and El Gran Capitán the new Spanish army had fallen. Between 1635 and 1665 the Portuguese fought themselves free of Spain. At the same time, adding to Spain's troubles, there was a fierce though unsuccessful revolt of the Catalans, who wanted to reaffirm or even extend their old autonomy.

Against this increasingly dismal back cloth, the Spanish Empire remained the largest in the world, covering all of southern Italy as well as the huge mineral-bearing stretches of the Americas. The aim of the Spanish government was to populate the New World, to bring back its wealth and to evangelize. Emigration was officially restricted to Roman Catholics of good character. Figures are difficult to establish, but by the end of the 18th Century, according to Humboldt, the scientist-explorer, there were 18.8 million persons, including natives, in the Spanish colonies, of whom 1.9 million were in the Philippines.

The Spanish government began to be preoccupied with mounting discontent in the colonies, either by separatists or by natives. It was no wonder in these circumstances that the other more powerful nations of Europe—notably Britain and France—came to look on Spain as a dying monarchy whose rich possessions they would soon be able to gather to themselves.

THE last of the Spanish Hapsburgs, the sickly, dull-witted Charles II, was a symbol of the fading empire. Obviously fated to die without children, he passed his whole reign witnessing a squabble between the likely successors to his dominions and their international backers. Within two years of his death in 1700, a general European war broke out for the Spanish succession. The contenders were Philip of Anjou, who had been named by Charles II as his successor, and Charles of Austria, heir to the crown of the Holy Roman Empire. Philip was backed by France (Louis XIV was his grandfather) and Charles by England and Austria. In time, Philip secured the throne, although the long years of war resulted in Spain's surrender to Austria of most of its Italian possessions and the loss of Gibraltar to England.

Philip V began the rule of the Spanish Bourbons, who were even more absolutist than the Hapsburgs had been. He was immediately faced with a new separatist uprising in Catalonia. The War of the Succession was turned into a civil war that ended with defeat for the Catalans and destruction of their hopes for independence.

The rule of the Spanish Bourbons (1701-1808) was dominated externally by a series of foreign wars, arising partly from the ambitions of the kings or their wives to get back the European territory lost in the War of the Spanish Succession, and partly because of English piracy around the margins of the Spanish Empire. Internally, the period was characterized by attempts of the Bourbon monarchs to centralize the power of the state.

CHARLES III was one of Spain's best kings. During his reign (1759-1788), the Jesuits were expelled and the country at least attempted economic reforms. Nevertheless, in late 18th Century Spain, dire, continuous poverty prevailed throughout most of Castile, Aragon and La Mancha. Vast holdings of land were concentrated in the hands of the nobles and the Church. There were few small farmers, and the absentee landlord was the rule.

The final blow to the old Spanish governmental system came as a result of the French Revolution, which brought from across the border first of all new ideas, then French arms. The French revolutionary government's rough treatment of the French king naturally incurred the hostility of his Bourbon kinsman, Charles IV of Spain. After a period of groveling concessions to Napoleon, the Spanish king and his son were persuaded in 1808 to abdicate. A French army under Joachim Murat occupied Madrid, and Napoleon established his brother, Joseph Bonaparte, on the throne of Spain. But Napoleon had reckoned without the feelings of the Spanish people. In a demonstration of passionate outrage, the Spaniards asserted themselves as a united nation. There was a general uprising against the French invaders. What followed has been continually tumultuous, and is still unsettled. As the great Spanish novelist Benito Pérez Galdós has put it: "In 1808 the Spanish people left home: they have not yet returned." Pérez Galdós was writing in the late 19th Century. But his words apply with equal accuracy to the 1960s.

NOBLEMAN'S STUDY containing more than 10,000 volumes *(left)* is part of a palace built in Majorca by the Marquis of Vivot in the 18th Century. Like other lordly houses it is decorated with tapestries and frescoed walls.

MAGNIFICENT LIBRARY in the Escorial, the overwhelming Renaissance palace built by Philip II in the 16th Century *(opposite)*, gleams with brilliant frescoes and marble floors. It contains many priceless manuscripts.

A Flood Tide of Influence and Its Ebb

Spain had a brilliant morning and noonday of power. First, to exploit the Americas, Spain's galleons brought home vast treasures of gold. Through dynastic marriages Spain's monarchs could lay claim to possessions all over Europe.

Spanish arms were for a while victorious everywhere. The climax came in the 16th Century, when the huge Escorial palace was built and the Armada sailed against England. But even as Spain seemed supreme, its power began to ebb.

THE "INVINCIBLE ARMADA," which set out to destroy British sea power, is shown in the harbor of Calais in 1588, being attacked by fire ships sent in from a crescent of pursuing British warships *(right)*. The ungainly Spanish ships were driven out into the North Sea where the British sank scores of them. Many of the rest met ruin on

the stormy coasts of Scotland and Ireland. Only half the great fleet ever reached home. The foolhardy venture was inspired partly by religious fervor—hatred of England's Protestantism—and partly as the answer to England's interfering with Spanish holdings in the Low Countries. After the defeat, Spain never recovered its former power.

A NOBLEWOMAN *echoes in patrician ways the age when Spain was supreme*

DECORATIVE RIDING HABIT, including embossed leather chaps, is worn by the stately Duchess of Alba as she prepares to lead a charity parade in Madrid. The heiress to some 57 titles, she owns four castles in Spain, hundreds of paintings by such artists as Titian and Rembrandt, and farmlands so vast that their acreage is secret.

ELEGANT CARRIAGE transports the duchess and a companion home from the Seville bull ring. As a onetime *rejoneadora*, she has herself fought bulls from horseback.

SUPERB PAINTINGS, including the famous Goya portrait of the thirteenth Duchess of Alba, deck the Madrid palace where the present duchess poses with her five sons.

In a scene of the 1930s, Seville children play in the ruins of a building destroyed by bombs. The shattered walls and the crippled

child suggest the agony that racked Spain in the Civil War.

4

Decline

and

Disaster

THE Spanish Civil War of 1936-1939 was the tragic result of 130 years of political false starts, bloodshed, selfish decisions and fresh false starts. The war amounted to an admission that Spain had failed to settle any of its major national problems. These problems have recurred again and again in Spanish history like dominant themes in a discordant symphony.

Ever since the collapse of the absolute monarchy in 1808, three separate, bitter struggles have gone on in Spain. First, the traditionalists (including the Church) have fought with the liberal reformers, who wanted free elections, a free press and lay education. Second, the economically advanced sections of the country have continued to resist control from Madrid. Finally, the working class, anxious to achieve self-respect and security, has struggled against a landowning upper class which has not been interested in—or has refused to understand— the working man's problems. The Civil War was thus three wars in one: it was a war of ideas, a war of secession and a class war. It was also a war in which both sides, with strange allies, mistakenly believed that they could achieve a renaissance of Spain's golden past through a revolution that would wipe out the failures and political mismanagement of centuries.

DURING the 19th Century, Spain lost nearly all its colonies, but its rulers continued to live in a dream world of empire. Actually, Spain itself during this time gradually became a financial semicolony of Europe. The companies that grew out of foreign investments took over Spain's railway construction, gasworks, mines and railways. About two thirds of the Spanish people in mid-century depended for a living, under miserable conditions of poverty, on the land. Yet liberal politicians, aware of the sad plight of agricultural workers, could not establish communications with a people who were dominated by the ideological thinking of the Church and the wealthy landowners.

The bloodshed began in 1808, when the people rose against the French occupation forces and the French-imposed king, Joseph Bonaparte. The date of the uprising, Dos de Mayo (May 2), is still celebrated throughout the country. There was much colorful guerrilla warfare by the Spaniards and a glorious battle (fought at Bailén in Andalusia) where untrained Spanish peasants overwhelmed a trained French force. Nonetheless, victory in the ensuing war of independence (the Peninsular War) was won only with English assistance, led by the Duke of Wellington. During the conflict, Spain returned to local patriotisms: the mayor of the village of Móstoles, for example, declared war directly against Napoleon. It was also a time of a nationalistic spirit of redemption, for this war of independence was a great occasion of national self-consciousness celebrated with many songs and anecdotes.

The final victory over the French in 1814 ushered in a new false start: Spain once again tried a monarchy and adopted a brave statement of liberal principles called the Constitution of Cadiz. The old Bourbon crown prince

was freed by Napoleon and returned to the Spanish throne as King Ferdinand VII. The constitution was framed in 1812, while the war was still in progress, by a *cortes* of liberals who —unhappy and expressive portent for the future—had very little contact with the common men who were still waging guerrilla warfare against the French. The constitution was based on all the leading liberal ideas of the day—including the disentailment of the great estates, the seizing of church property, the abolition of the Inquisition, guarantees for free speech, free elections and freedom of education.

The struggle for a constitution along these lines has continued ever since, and it was a central issue in the ideological tension that brought on the Civil War. King Ferdinand received an ovation when he arrived in Valencia and apparently felt that his popularity was so great that he could afford to shove the constitution aside. The liberals who had framed the constitution were shot, imprisoned or fled into exile abroad.

AFTER six years there was a reaction. In 1820 the army, led by Colonel Rafael del Riego, forced the king to re-establish the constitution. The "men of 1812" were welcomed back. But bickering among the members of the new government—a typical source of liberal failures—gave the king an opportunity to appeal to his foreign allies for help. The ambassadors of France, Austria, Prussia and Russia (all reactionary governments) presented notes to the Spanish government demanding the abolition of the constitution. The government refused, and the ambassadors left Madrid. Thereupon, a French army—"the 100,000 sons of St. Louis"—invaded Spain and restored Ferdinand to the pretensions of his ancestors. The invasion was not resisted by the Spanish people, and this suggests that the liberals did not really have popular support. Riego was executed.

After that, the liberals suffered persecution for a decade. They were gradually eased back into the government by Ferdinand's widow, María Cristina, on behalf of her daughter, the infant Queen Isabella. But this was the signal for a new conflict. The infant queen's claim to the throne was disputed by her uncle, Don Carlos, Ferdinand's brother, who denied the right of females to succeed to the throne.

The ferocious Carlist Wars that ensued were fought with bitterness and violence all over northern Spain. Although the liberal supporters of the still-infant Queen Isabella eventually won, their victory was pyrrhic: they were unable to restore the Constitution of Cadiz, and their only outstanding achievement was taking away, in 1836, the Church's lands—which were immediately bought up by profiteers. The rich got richer, and the poor got poorer.

Spain was by this time no longer a world empire. The example of the successful revolt of Britain's American colonies, the errors of Spanish officialdom, the highhanded attitude that Spain took toward the aspirations of the colonists for more say in their own government— all these reasons contributed to the colonial drive for independence. Furthermore, Spain had been losing contact with its colonies ever since the Battle of Trafalgar in 1805, when Horatio Nelson's victory for Britain over the combined French and Spanish fleets destroyed Spain's power at sea. In 1810 there was an uprising in Venezuela. Between then and 1824 other parts of Spanish America fought their way to freedom. By 1825, Cuba, Puerto Rico and the Philippines were practically all that remained of Spain's imperial dominions.

THE first Carlist Wars ended with a compromise peace at Vergara in 1839 by which Isabella's claim to the throne was recognized, but—through a *muy español* agreement—all the officers of the defeated Carlist army were taken into the Spanish army at their old rank. The army was becoming the strongest institution of the Spanish state, and the crown was never to recover from its ignominious abdication in the wars against Napoleon.

For the next 35 years (1840-1875) the army dictated Spanish politics, and *pronunciamientos* (coups d'état) were the normal method whereby a conservative general seized control of the government from a liberal general. The remainder of the reign of Queen Isabella II went on in a murky atmosphere of plot and counterplot, while the nymphomaniac queen herself passed from lover to lover—and became an object of either outrage or laughter to her enemies.

During these years, another of the profound conflicts in Spanish society began to manifest itself: the working class showed signs of becoming conscious that it was being badly governed. Throughout the countryside there was misery and near-starvation. Industrial activity was getting off to a slow start, except in Catalonia and the Basque Provinces. An outburst of church burning occurred in the middle of the 1830s. From that time on there was a good deal of aimless banditry in Andalusia, prompting the government to establish a special rural police force, the now-famous Guardia Civil.

IN 1868 the continuing personal irresponsibility of Queen Isabella led to her expulsion as "insupportable." A democratic monarchial constitution was proclaimed, and a search for a new king began. Prince Amadeo of Savoy, brother of the king of Italy, was eventually chosen, but he was unable to make anything out of a situation in which the self-governing aspirations of the Spanish provinces began to reassert themselves.

For a while, all the main cities along the Mediterranean coast, in protest against the disorder radiating from Madrid, were in a state of semi-independence under local juntas. The Carlists in Navarre took up arms again under the leadership of a grandson of the first Don Carlos.

Finally, in 1868 there arrived in Madrid the first apostle from the International Brotherhood ("in politics anarchist, in economy collectivist, in religion atheist") to spread the ideas of the Russian anarchist Michael Bakunin to a delighted group of Madrid printers. Within a few years this new "international" movement—as the anarchists were first known—had gathered some 50,000 members.

All these signs of total dissolution were too much for King Amadeo, and he abdicated in

1873. The first Spanish Republic that followed was led by a group of federally minded intellectuals. They had the highest intentions, but were powerless to control the aspirations of either the regionalists or the working class. Finally the army took over once again and restored Isabella's son (who was reputedly illegitimate) as King Alfonso XII. At the same time the army launched another campaign against the Carlists, and for a while succeeded in quieting them.

THE restoration which brought in Alfonso offered a new chance for the peaceful development of Spain. Universal suffrage was respected for a while. But the great opportunity soon began to disappear. The power of corrupt local bosses *(caciques)* turned the struggle between conservatives and liberals into a charade. The working class had no possibility of gaining political power. At about the same time, there were stirrings of a new regionalism in Catalonia—but this time it was mostly a literary revival of the Catalan language and culture. This renaissance was encouraged by the industrial development of the region and the rising irritation of new European-minded businessmen with the government of Madrid.

Some of the working class, known both for its extreme idealism and for its willingness to accept violence, began now to embrace Bakunin's anarchistic formula as if it were a new religion. Militant anarchists traveled around the villages of Andalusia like wandering friars, and the exciting word spread like wildfire. The landless were learning in their long months of unemployment to read, to give up tobacco and even coffee—all in the great new cause. In 1910 a general union was formed, the Confederación Nacional del Trabajo (National Confederation of Labor, or CNT).

Throughout the first two decades of the 20th Century, the anarchists became more and more violent. There were revolts and political murders in Barcelona. A branch of the international Socialist movement also made some headway. These two working-class movements, totally misunderstood by the upper classes, developed against a background of increasing misery, overpopulation and 50 per cent illiteracy.

The continuing crises that eventually ended in the debacle of 1936 shook every segment of Spanish society for more than a century. Faction warred against faction. No political group seemed able to agree with any other group on how the country should be run. No political salvage operation worked out. The monarchy's troubles began to come to a head in 1885 when Alfonso XII died at the age of 28 and was succeeded by his posthumous son Alfonso XIII, whose regent was the Queen Mother María Cristina. A renewed Cuban war of independence in 1895 gave birth to the Spanish-American War. Cuba won its independence, and the Philippines and Puerto Rico were ceded to the United States. Spain's American empire was gone. An intellectual movement tried to arouse Spain to adjust itself economically and to face the future instead of dreaming about the past: "We must double-lock the sepulchre of the Cid," pleaded the jurist, Joaquín Costa, a leading representative of the "generation of '98."

The defeats in Cuba gave to the Spanish army an embittered sense of grievance at what they regarded as mismanagement at home. The army thought of itself as a symbol of order in an unstable society, and among the officers there was an increasing willingness to undertake political action. In 1909 an uprising in Morocco against the Spanish protectorate there triggered a war that lasted almost continuously until 1927. It was a war that gave army officers every opportunity to obtain battle experience (if they survived), to grumble at political mismanagement and to win swift promotion. The Moroccan wars were accompanied by wave upon wave of internal uprisings, each one shaking the country more fiercely than the last.

WORLD WAR I brought new complications. Spain remained outside the conflict, but was divided between adherents of Germany and of the Allies. Prosperity increased, but prices rose. The Russian Revolution inspired vast enthusiasm throughout the working class.

In 1917 the increasingly powerful Socialist party and its affiliated trade union, the Unión General de Trabajadores (General Union of Workers, or UGT), as strong in Madrid as the anarchists were in Barcelona, declared a general strike. While the central government dithered, the strike was crushed by the army.

THE parliamentary system never recovered. Governments came and went with monotonous regularity. For five or six years after the strike, Barcelona was the scene of almost continuous street fighting between the anarchists and stool pigeon trade unionists allied with the police. Political murders continued.

The Socialist party meantime refused to affiliate with the new (third) Communist International. A small section of Socialists (with some disaffected anarchists) thereupon broke away to found the Spanish Communist party—which was insignificant for some time. Finally, Alfonso, an intelligent man but a meddler in politics, committed a fatal mistake by encouraging a reckless general in Morocco to start a campaign that ended in the virtual extermination of the Spanish army. The inevitable parliamentary inquiry was expected to incriminate the crown. And so the king made no opposition when the Captain General of Catalonia, General Miguel Primo de Rivera, carried out a 19th Century type of *pronunciamiento* in the name of order.

Primo de Rivera ruled as dictator from 1923 to 1930, nominally under the king. He fancied himself the Spanish Mussolini, and his economic policy (public works, cheap money, industrial expansion) seemed fascistic. But Primo de Rivera was hard-working and personally engaging. A wenching, hard-drinking Andalusian, he was wildly popular in spite of his authoritarianism. His most outstanding achievements were to bring about, with French help, a successful end to the Moroccan wars and to maintain a remarkably peaceful administration in contrast to the turbulence of preceding years.

Primo de Rivera fell from power in 1930 because the world economic depression brought about the collapse of his economic policy, because his censorship outraged the intellectuals and because he lost the support of the army officers who had brought him to power.

Primo de Rivera's fall, however, left the king with no backing and no means of forming a government. A caretaker administration of admirals and generals was gathered together. But by now the king was opposed by much of the Church, by the army and, of course, by the urban working classes and professional people. He therefore decided to leave Spain (to avoid a civil war, he said)—although he was careful not to abdicate formally. The government was taken over in a mood of euphoria by a Republican alliance of middle-class liberals and Socialists.

The second Republic began in 1931. Its principal leader was the liberal, Manuel Azaña; his government immediately tried to carry out all the reforms, administrative and social, which Spain so desperately needed if it was to become even a limitedly liberal country along the modest lines of France or Britain. Thus the government tried to exile the Jesuits, to separate Church and state, to destroy the Church's control of education, to provide a whole new system and climate of education, to take the army out of politics, to establish modern labor conditions, to give autonomy to Catalonia and afterwards to Galicia and the Basque Provinces, and to carry out an effective agrarian reform.

THIS program, especially with the priority unwisely given to religious questions, inevitably alienated all practicing Catholics. Monarchist plots sprang up. Fascist groups grew under the influence of Italy and Germany. The government had enemies on Right and Left. Although backed by the Socialists, the Republic had never been accepted by the million and a half anarchists whose chief bases were still in Andalusia and Barcelona. They found the reforms of the government far too moderate.

Within a month of the establishment of the Republic, the churches of many leading cities were set on fire. There were numerous strikes and local riots. In 1933, the village of Casas

Viejas rose against the Guardia Civil—apparently expecting a general strike that would lead to the millennium. The rebels were put down in a merciless blood bath.

The first period of Republican government (1931-1933) turned into a shambles, dominated by an ineffective combination of politicians of the Center and the Left. Azaña fell from power. There were incessant strikes, including a long general strike in Saragossa. The Catalan autonomous government declared itself the federal republic of Catalonia, and the miners of Asturias rose in armed revolt.

E VERYWHERE except in Asturias this revolution was soon defeated and its ringleaders silenced. In Asturias, the Socialist miners (supported by both anarchists and a few Communists) set up a revolutionary government of their own. This revolt was crushed only by the arrival of the Foreign Legion and Moorish troops, led by the cleverest and youngest of the generals who had distinguished themselves in Morocco, General Francisco Franco.

The uprising itself and its repression shook the whole of Spanish society. The middle and upper classes were aghast at the prospect of their own total eclipse. The working class had won a taste of actual mastery and also a heroic rallying cry. After 1934 it would have been almost impossible to work out a compromise that would have prevented a civil war.

In February 1936 a new election gave a decisive electoral vote to an alliance of Socialists, Liberals and Communists (organized according to the Popular Front principles blessed the previous year in Moscow by the Seventh Congress of the Comintern). In this election, many anarchists also voted for the first time, and with the Left. Azaña returned to power, although this time no Socialists would take office. Their leader, Largo Caballero, fancied himself, because of Communist flattery, "the Spanish Lenin" and opposed the idea of taking office again in a "bourgeois" cabinet. Street fighting continued, and the young Fascists of the small, recently formed Falange movement, headed by José

Antonio Primo de Rivera, a son of the old dictator, deliberately took advantage of the revolutionary situation.

Strikes occurred every day, and there were 230 political murders and countermurders between February and July, along with 160 church burnings. The weak liberal government pressed ahead with reforms; Azaña claimed that during 1936 some 75,000 peasants were settled on land in Estremadura. An increasingly large section of landowners and traditionalists began to feel that they would be swept away by the great tides of leftism. Conscious of this feeling, a number of right-wing generals began to make serious preparations for a military coup and established relations with veteran monarchist plotters and with the recently reinvigorated Carlists who, still supporting a candidate of the old Carlist line for the throne of Spain, were training militia in the hills of Navarre.

The Civil War began in July. The army set out to take power from a government which they charged could not keep order. The generals were backed by the Carlists, the orthodox monarchists, the rich landowners, most of the Church, some of the middle class and ultimately the Fascists of the Falange—although the Falange leaders had reservations about supporting what they considered a reactionary cause. Against them were ranged the Republican government, the workers, some of the middle class, and a scattered assortment of Liberals, Socialists and Communists.

T HE officers in charge of garrisons proclaimed a state of war and swooped down on the towns to establish martial law. The uprising was successful in Morocco and in the main cities of Andalusia, Galicia, Aragon and Old Castile. In all cases there was fighting in which many workers and other opponents of the uprising (including many loyal officers) were killed. In Madrid, Barcelona, Bilbao, Valencia and throughout many country districts in the south, the working-class movements successfully resisted the army uprising and staged their own revolution by burning churches, killing

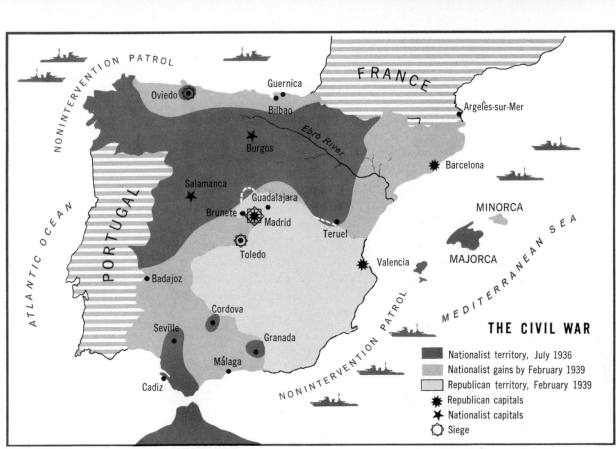

The Civil War map labels:

NONINTERVENTION PATROL

FRANCE

ATLANTIC OCEAN

PORTUGAL

MEDITERRANEAN SEA

Oviedo • Guernica •
Bilbao •
Ebro River
Argelès-sur-Mer
Burgos ★
Barcelona ✸
Salamanca ★
Guadalajara
Brunete • Madrid
Teruel •
MINORCA
Toledo •
Valencia ✸
MAJORCA
Badajoz •
Cordova •
Seville •
Granada •
Málaga •
Cadiz •

NONINTERVENTION PATROL

THE CIVIL WAR

- Nationalist territory, July 1936
- Nationalist gains by February 1939
- Republican territory, February 1939
- ✸ Republican capitals
- ★ Nationalist capitals
- ⬡ Siege

SHIFTING BATTLE LINES of the Civil War are shown here. The war began in July 1936 with Nationalist (Rebel) uprisings in the northwest and south. Later that summer, with the capture of Badajoz, the two areas were linked. Republican (Loyalist) holdouts in the north were subdued in a 1937 campaign which included a terroristic bombing of Guernica. In the next year and a half the Nationalists gained steadily, although the Republicans temporarily won back some territory (dotted lines) and for a while regained Teruel. Nationalist capitals were at Salamanca and Burgos; the Republican capital was at Madrid, then Valencia, then Barcelona. Ships of various countries ineffectually patrolled the coastlines. In 1938 the Nationalists reached the Mediterranean, and by early 1939, after fierce fighting along the Ebro River, they had taken the whole northeast, and Republican refugees began fleeing out to the Argelès-sur-Mer area in France. The war ended with Madrid's capture in March 1939.

priests, and taking over political and economic control in the territory they held. The bloodletting on both sides was enormous.

As actual warfare began, the army held the territory it had won by martial law and marched on Madrid with a motley collection of volunteers and regular soldiers. The government, with the help of the working classes, began to dispatch militiamen drawn from the unions to meet the army. The two sides called themselves Republicans (or Loyalists) and Nationalists. To their enemies they were known as Reds and Fascists. The war resulted in about 100,000 deaths in battle and 10,000 in air raids. There were perhaps 220,000 murders and executions. At least 50,000 more died from hunger and disease. After the army triumph, close to 200,000 Loyalist prisoners were shot or died of disease in prison cells. More than 300,000 exiles left Spain forever.

There were three specific reasons for the army victory. First, General Franco had more and better up-to-date war materials furnished by Germany, Italy and Portugal, in contrast to the sporadic flow of materials sent to the Republicans by Russia, Mexico and, very occasionally, France. The backers of neither side dared allow their protégés to lose, but neither did they dare commit enough forces to enable their protégés to win—for fear of risking a general European war. As a consequence, whenever either side seemed on the verge of losing, its international champions would do their best to stem the tide. The war was thus prolonged. Britain and

France, followed by the United States, tried to prevent the intervention of foreign powers in Spain—but this policy simply assisted the army and harmed the Republic. Franco's final victorious campaign in Catalonia was made possible by a large consignment of war materials from Germany, at a time when the Republican forces were depleted and when it was almost impossible to get foreign arms into Republican territory, even if these had been available. The French had shut the frontier, and the Italians prevented Russian ships from crossing the Mediterranean to aid the Republicans.

The second cause of the army's victory was General Franco's skill in forging a political unity out of the disparate forces supporting him. None of the other generals could rival him either in political finesse or in general strategic judgment. The Falange grew in numbers and power during the Civil War, but the deaths of nearly all of its original leaders (including José Antonio Primo de Rivera) prevented it from being a serious rival to Franco. The Carlists, although they provided some of Franco's best fighters, were never in a position to impose their scheme of an absolute monarchy on a working-class society.

ON the Republican side, no such unity was created out of the alliance of anarchists, Communists and Socialists (themselves divided into several groups), semi-Trotskyists, old-fashioned liberals, and Catalan and Basque regionalists. The liberal government of the first days of the war gave way to a coalition led by the Socialist Largo Caballero, who had both anarchist and Communist ministers. This government in turn fell, and a university professor of physiology, Dr. Juan Negrín, acted as prime minister until the end of the war. Meanwhile, both Catalonia and the Basque Provinces experienced short periods of self-government.

By the end of the war the Communists had grown into one of the most powerful parties among the Republicans; they had the prestige of Russian aid, they had superior discipline and they were shrewd enough to advocate only moderate political reforms until the war was won. The prestige (and prowess) of the 40,000 Communist-led volunteers in the International Brigade also helped.

The disciplined political moderation of the Communists, however, caused incessant tension with the anarchists, and on two occasions it brought about large-scale fighting. The second of these battles, in March 1939, at the end of the war, was aimed at achieving a compromise peace. The move was successful in overthrowing Dr. Negrín and his Communist advisers who, in default of minimum guarantees against reprisals, were bent on fighting on to the end. The ensuing anarchist-liberal junta failed to gain any terms at all from General Franco, who by that time had an easy task in disposing of his divided opponents.

The third main cause of Franco's victory was his superior economic resources. He began by controlling half the territory in Spain, with most of the wheat- and meat-producing areas, but only a third of the population. He had far fewer people to feed than the disorganized Republicans, although they held the main industrial cities and the Spanish gold reserve. Franco secured a dependable oil supply through the credits of the Texas Corporation, and the German government was instrumental in bolstering the Nationalist currency. By the end of the war the Republican central zone was starving, its currency worthless, its war industries at a standstill and its gold reserve sent to the Soviet Union in payment for supplies.

THE end came in March 1939 with the complete victory of centralism against regional autonomy, of the Church against intellectual freedom and of the landowning class against the workers. The length of the hostilities made this "settlement" of the three major tensions in Spanish affairs especially brutal and made the hatreds it inspired more lasting. Among the approximately 250,000 Spaniards who have remained in exile—primarily in France, the United States, Mexico and Argentina—the fires of conflict have continued to burn.

In Robert Capa's famous picture, a Loyalist infantryman falls backward, shot through the head during the 1936 attack on Cordova.

The Interminable Agony of Civil War

The Spanish Civil War was one of the most savage conflicts in history. As many as 580,000 people are thought to have lost their lives. The world watched, appalled, as bombing of civilians was used for the first time on a large scale as a weapon of terror. But the war had a deeper significance, for it engaged the participation of Fascist Italy and Nazi Germany on one side and of Soviet Russia on the other, and thus served as a diabolical preview of World War II.

THE ARMIES, *often ragged and ill-armed, fiercely contested each town and hill*

LOYALIST DEFENDERS of Madrid fire from behind a barricade made largely of luggage obtained from a railroad station. Madrid was held by the Loyalists until 1939.

REBEL VICTORS in the north in 1936 patrol the streets of Irún, on the French border, looking for hidden Loyalists. When found, the Loyalists were usually shot down.

LOYALIST SQUAD, which includes one woman, defends a lightly fortified hillside position near Madrid. Many women fought with the Loyalist militia early in the war.

*WARTIME FERVOR ran high,
especially in the larger urban centers
where Loyalist strength lay*

SACKED CHURCH of San Miguel in Toledo was destroyed by a Loyalist mob. In their hatred for the conservative Church, the Loyalists shot thousands of priests and nuns.

ANXIOUS REFUGEES in Barcelona watch a rebel bomber overhead. Both Germany and Italy supplied Franco with aircraft and crews, overwhelming the Loyalist air force.

CIVILIAN PARADE in Barcelona in January 1938 celebrates Loyalist successes at Teruel. But later heavy losses at Teruel contributed to the Loyalists' eventual defeat.

DETERMINED TROOPS march in Valencia in the summer of 1938. The Loyalist militia became an effective army late in the war, but could not resist Franco's final offensives.

ENTERING MADRID after nearly three years of assault, Franco's troops march through the Plaza de la Cibeles. Italian troops were given a place of honor in the parade.

LINING UP IN JAIL, some of the 240,000 Loyalists still behind bars in 1942 prepare to attend Mass. Executions of Loyalists were estimated at 1,000 a month in 1939.

FLEEING INTO FRANCE, refugees cross a stone bridge in the Pyrenees in 1939. Hundreds of thousands came through here although many froze to death on the way.

WAR'S END found Spain exhausted,

embittered and crippled by grievous wounds that were to take many years to heal

5

The Strong Man

GENERAL FRANCO'S regime has enjoyed absolute power since 1939. Its achievements are still debatable. It has maintained external peace and internal order; it inspired an industrial expansion in the 1950s and 1960s; and under its rule a middle class has begun to develop which may eventually bridge the hitherto unbridgeable gap between rich and poor.

There are also reasons for condemning the Franco regime. It has maintained a rigorous censorship of most of the means of communication; it has banned freedom of political expression and the right of students and others to form their own representative associations;

it has done little to alleviate the condition of life in the Spanish countryside; it has made no clear provision for the future of the country; and it has not yet really changed the historic division of Spain into two parts—rich and poor—which know little of each other. Politically, Spain is a complete question mark, and no one, Left or Right, is able to give a confident answer to the question as to what would happen if the Strong Man should disappear or die.

The character of General Franco has dominated the regime. He is the product of a middle-class family which settled in Galicia. Most of his immediate forebears were in the navy. Francisco Franco Bahamonde had been scheduled for a navy career, but Spain's naval academy was closed for a time after the disastrous Spanish-American War, and he went into the army instead. Soon he was in Morocco (1912). He became known as an outstanding leader with a strong tactical and strategic sense, a man brave under fire, a "puritanical" soldier not given to gambling and wenching. He was active (along with Lieutenant Colonel José Millán Astray) in the organization of the Spanish Foreign Legion—on the French model—and took an outstanding part in the fighting against the Riffs.

THE youngest general in the Spanish army at 32, as he had been the youngest captain and colonel, Franco was known as a dedicated soldier. His politics were more uncertain, although it was fairly clear that he was of an authoritarian frame of mind. Franco was head of the military academy at Saragossa at the time of the fall of the monarchy in 1931. He was cold-shouldered by the left-wing Republican governments and was used by the right-wing faction in 1934 to crush the rising of the Asturian miners. In 1936 he flew from the Canary Islands to take command of the rebelling Spanish troops in Morocco, and it was his skill which led both to the success of the early campaigns of the Civil War and to the rebels' success in gaining foreign aid. He emerged from the war as *Caudillo* (leader) and head of state, with a reputation and prestige that none of the other generals or leaders could rival.

During the Civil War, many of Franco's keenest supporters had thought that he would restore the monarchy. But as the years went by it became clear, to the annoyance of many of his old comrades, that there were endless possibilities of procrastination. And, in fact, General Franco has continued to rule ever since the Civil War by using a brand of compromise, evolved during the conflict, between the Church (which has dominant influence over the educational and cultural life of the country), the Falange (Spain's only political party, which has devel-

oped into a large bureaucracy with few of its social aspirations remaining) and the army—upon which Franco relies for maintenance of order; top-ranking officers are often members of Franco's cabinet. Most political opponents have been tried by military courts.

Against this pattern, General Franco's rule has gone through several distinct periods. The first lasted from April 1939 until late in 1942; this was the time when the Axis powers seemed likely to win the general European war. During this period, therefore, Franco kept close to the Axis political position and agreed to join Germany on condition that Spain be given Gibraltar, the whole of French Morocco and Oran, together with enough stores of war materials to enable Spain to withstand any British attack. These terms were unacceptable to the Germans, who felt that the Axis had already given Franco too much without reward. The negotiations continued endlessly, with Franco's brother-in-law and foreign minister, Serrano Suñer, as the chief advocate of the Axis alliance inside Spain. The closest Spain eventually came to joining Germany was to send its Blue Division to fight against Russia from 1941 to 1943.

Internally, this first period of Franco's rule was unrelieved tragedy, beginning with a vast number of imprisonments and executions. The precise total of the latter is incalculable, but about 200,000 Loyalist prisoners either died before firing squads or perished from disease between 1939 and 1943. Great shortages caused by the Civil War could not be made good during the world war. The year 1941 was one of maximum hardship in Spain because of plague and famine: many people died of hunger.

DURING the second half of World War II, General Franco tried to make adjustments with the Allied powers, while they in turn did their best to court him. The Allies wanted to prevent a close Spanish alignment with Germany, which might have jeopardized the success of the North African campaign. It was also understood that Britain and the United States would continue to supply oil to Spain, but that Spain would not supply iron and other war materials to Germany.

At the end of the war, the regime received several harsh blows. First, the monarchists, led by the Pretender Don Juan (ex-King Alfonso XIII had died in Rome in 1941), issued in March 1945 a liberal manifesto causing a sharp breach between the regime and the monarchists. At the same time, a group of underground fighters who had successfully made war on the Germans began an anti-Franco campaign in the Pyrenees. Guerrilla warfare lasted sporadically until 1948, and isolated banditry continued until the 1950s. Meanwhile, the powers forming the new United Nations in 1945 decided to exclude Spain from the organization, and in early 1946 Poland took the lead in the U.N. to demand the end of the Franco regime.

IN an attempt to gain popularity, Franco in July 1945 issued a so-called declaration of human rights (Fuero de los Españoles), and in September of that year came such conciliatory gestures to the Allies as the easing of a 1937 law obliging officials and military personnel to use the Fascist salute on ceremonial occasions. Both the United States and Britain opposed the U.N. move against Spain. Nevertheless, at the end of 1946 the U.N. General Assembly, by a large majority which included the United States and Britain, recommended that member states recall their ambassadors from Madrid. Britain, France and the United States had declared that their aim was to achieve the "peaceful withdrawal of Franco, the abolition of the Falange, and the establishment of an interim or caretaker government under which the Spanish people may have an opportunity freely to determine the type of government they wish to have." General Franco made a rousing speech to a large crowd in Madrid in which he announced Spain's determination to stand alone in the face of these insults.

It now seems certain that the United Nations gesture was a mistake—especially since in a few years the U.N. was to reverse its stand. Further, Don Juan de Borbón, Pretender to the Spanish throne, felt that the U.N. move kept him from pressing forward with his plans for a constitutional monarchy. Many of the Pretender's supporters, understanding that their own fate was now inextricably bound to the *Caudillo's*, rallied to Franco's side. The economic embargo accompanying the U.N. decision was withstood with assistance from General Franco's brother dictator, Juan Perón of Argentina.

In a new attempt to gain popular backing and at the same time deflect the monarchists, Franco in 1947 announced a law of succession declaring Spain a "Catholic social and representative state which in accordance with its tradition" formed itself into a kingdom. Since then Spain has remained technically a kingdom—without a king. The future monarch must be male, a Spaniard of royal blood and at least 30 years old. (Don Juan was consulted about this matter when it was too late for him to make any effective suggestions.)

Some months later, in July of 1947, a referendum was held to endorse the spirit of this law. Some 13 million people voted, with 12 million coming out in favor of a monarchy, 643,000 voting against it and 320,000 turning in empty or spoiled ballots.

The United States now went back on its previous support of the 1946 U.N. resolution—partly because of cold war necessities, partly out of boredom with World War II issues, partly as a result of political pressures inside the United States government. The United States, nevertheless, under pressure from Britain and France, refused to back the entry of Spain into the Marshall Plan—which Spain had been expecting.

DESPITE all this, Spain's international stock was on the upswing. A Spanish agent arrived in the United States in April 1948, plunged headlong into the Washington social whirl and arranged a loan of $25 million to Spain. In May 1948 France allowed the resumption of trade between Spain and France, and Britain and the United States agreed with Spain on the liquidation of German holdings in the country. An American squadron was received with honor at

The Strong Man

El Ferrol in the autumn of 1949; in May 1950 the Chase Bank and the National City Bank gave a loan of $30 million to Spain; that fall the U.N. vote of 1946 was finally repealed, and the United States Congress made available to Spain a $62 million loan. In July 1951 Admiral Forrest Sherman, United States Chief of Naval Operations, visited Spain for preliminary discussion with Franco on the possibility of American bases in Spain. Two technical missions followed to deal with economic and military details.

The so-called 1953 Pact of Madrid between Spain and the United States constituted an agreement on bases, an agreement on U.S. assistance in modernizing Spain's armed forces and an economic aid agreement. The military aspects of the pact remain in force and are the chief link between Spain and the western

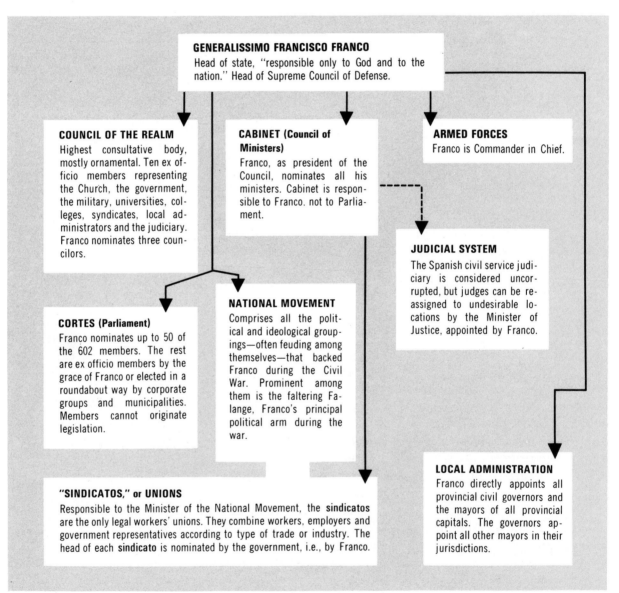

FRANCO'S POWER derives from his control, partial or complete, of virtually every organ of the Spanish government. Where he does not command outright, he has the power to wield a decisive influence. The solid lines in the chart above indicate the channels of his direct power; the dotted line a channel of less direct influence.

alliance as well as the chief element in Spanish foreign policy. The justification for the agreements in both Spanish and American eyes was, of course, the shared fear of communism. The defense agreement authorized the United States to develop and use, jointly with the Spanish government, certain bases which were to remain under Spanish sovereignty and under the "flag and command" of Spain.

Under the agreements, three major air bases were set up—at Torrejón, Morón and Saragossa—and an air force communications center at San Pablo, Seville. A naval base was established at Rota, near Cádiz, which has assumed vital importance as logistic headquarters of the U.S. Polaris submarine fleet in Europe. Two American tracking stations are now operating in Spain—one for tracking deep-space probes just north of Madrid, and a manned-flight tracking station in the Canary Islands.

The U.S. bases on Spanish soil are small colonies of the American way of life and isolated from all else. American servicemen do not wear uniforms off the base except in line of duty, and their multidenominational churches are not open to Spaniards. There has been little explicit Spanish criticism of the behavior of American personnel in Spain. But it would be naive to think that Americans are generally popular. There is surface cordiality, but an undercurrent of resentment. Students refer to American servicemen as the "army of occupation," and many Spanish liberals are convinced that the United States has kept Franco in power.

DURING the 1950s the Spanish economy received crucial support from the United States, which furnished Franco $400 million in military aid and $800 million in nonmilitary aid. But the new alliance has not been greeted with pleasure everywhere. In 1951 Britain's foreign secretary, Herbert Morrison, said that in the British view the "strategic advantages which might accrue from associating Spain with Western defence would be outweighed by the political damage." This view is still maintained by several NATO allies—though not by the British.

The gradual end of Spain's ostracism by the rest of the world (Spain was allowed into the United Nations in 1955) has undoubtedly assisted Franco in his internal political dealings, where the change from the 1945 position has naturally been hailed as a great achievement of Franco's political genius. In 1948 Franco undertook for the first time to meet Don Juan, the Pretender. The discussion, which took place on the yacht *Azor* off St. Sebastian, centered not only on the future of the regime but on the question of the education of Prince Juan Carlos, Don Juan's son. This has been an important question in Franco's relations with the monarchists ever since; the issue was whether the prince (supposed to be Franco's choice for a future king, in place of his father) should be educated at home or abroad.

THE upshot of the *Azor* meeting was the decision to have Don Juan Carlos educated mainly inside Spain, with tutors selected both by his father and by Franco. Franco has met Don Juan several times since then, and the two men have developed a reasonably cordial relationship. But Franco has never recognized Don Juan as the heir. The understandings arrived at in their meetings together have been couched in the vaguest possible terms, and it is probable that Franco would prefer to wait until Don Juan Carlos is 30 (in 1968) before committing himself about the future. Don Juan, who is Anglophile by inclination and education, clearly still has his private reservations about a full recognition of the Franco regime.

During the decade which passed immediately following the period of Spanish ostracism, the regime, with the impetus of American economic aid, pressed ahead with an ambitious industrialization plan while neglecting agricultural development. At the same time it continued to rely on agriculture (notably oranges and wine) for foreign exchange.

The consequence was that in 1958 Spain came close to bankruptcy and was thereupon forced to launch the stabilization plan of 1959, which froze wages and liberalized import and price controls. This plan, combined with the vast increase in the number of tourists flocking to Spain, succeeded in revolutionizing the foreign exchange situation within two years. By the middle of 1962 the Spanish gold reserves were higher than they had been at any point since the Civil War.

The successful stabilization plan was followed in the 1960s by an economic development plan that has brought about a further expansion of industry, with increased employment and higher living standards for workers *(Chapter 6)*. At the same time, a beginning has been made toward solving some of the age-old problems of the countryside. Today the nation's economic progress is creating a new middle class in at least the larger cities of the center and north—a scooter-riding, television- and football-conscious class such as has never previously existed in Spain. It is a class whose political weight remains to be seen.

POLITICALLY, the regime has not evolved noticeably since 1939. General Franco has remained and remains the effective autocrat. There is a cabinet, but its members are appointed by the Strong Man, and its periodic reshuffles have been dictated by General Franco's desire to have monarchist influence predominant at one time and Falangist at another time. The Spanish *cortes,* or parliament, is mostly an honorary group of appointed figureheads.

The main support of the regime is the armed forces. First there is the army itself, numbering about 250,000—a well-trained and efficient force which has been armed in recent years with American tanks, artillery pieces and ground-to-air missiles. The officers and noncoms are regulars, while the rank and file is made up of conscripts, most of whom serve for a period of 12 months. Secondly, there is the Guardia Civil, or Civil Guard, the police force in green uniforms and 18th Century black patent leather hats, which has existed since 1844 to keep order in the countryside and which is now probably about 30,000 strong. The navy numbers about 45,000, and the air force 38,000. Since the start of the American bases program, the air force has been strengthened by gifts of jet planes and pilot training in the United States. Franco also has at his disposal the Policía Armada, whose business is to keep order in the cities, an ordinary police force and a powerful political police force of an uncertain number.

ALL of these forces are kept up primarily to maintain order inside Spain. Since the Civil War, there has never been more than a whisper that any of these forces is disloyal to the regime, although a few of the leading generals of top rank have from time to time been suspected of personal ambitions. Some of them have also been too overtly monarchist for the discreet General Franco. The *esprit de corps* of the army seems to have been greatly increased since the conclusion of the alliance with the United States and the subsequent interchange of military training. However, there is some discontent at lower levels within the three services, chiefly because of the poor pay, which compels many officers to take second jobs in civilian life in order to make ends meet.

Next in importance to the military backing of the regime is the traditional, highly centralized civil administration organized under the Ministry of the Interior. Its appointed representative in each province is the civil governor. He presides over a small government of his own, although many of the central ministries maintain in each province their own representatives reporting directly to Madrid. The governor receives orders from Madrid, and his freedom of action is limited. Each province is divided into a series of *Partidos Judiciales,* or groups of small towns, the mayors of which join together to elect a *Diputación Provincial,* which forms the provincial government. The mayor of each town is chosen by the civil governor. He is in complete political control and is answerable only to the civil governor. The local instruments of government are thus stringently controlled from Madrid.

The Falange Española Tradicionalista y de las Juntas de Ofensiva Nacional-Sindicalista is the official name of the only political group that is permitted in Spain. The title is usually shortened to F.E.T. de las JONS, or simply to "the Falange." It is part of the "National Movement," and most government employees are members. It is based on the original Fascist party of the pre-Civil War era—although that group was not a mass party. In the Civil War, General Franco forced a merger of the Falangists with other splinter groups of the Right to form a single party. But it was the Falange that was the leading influence in the regime during the Civil War and immediate postwar years, although the pure and often sincere radicalism of the early Falangists had perished as surely as had most of its early leaders—in the fire of the Civil War.

MOST of the governments of Franco have had Falangist membership. But it is hard to think of the Falange as a serious bulwark of his regime. The few members of the movement today who retain any of their old-time radical views are probably in constant opposition; perhaps they even share the opinion of the young Falangist who startled everyone present by proclaiming Franco a traitor at the 1959 opening ceremony of the Civil War monument in the Valley of the Fallen. On the other hand, the vast majority of old Falangists have become middle-aged businessmen, profiting from the recent industrial successes and also from the more long-standing corruption and profiteering which have attended the Franco regime throughout much of its history.

Far more important than the party as a bulwark of the regime is its labor front, the official trade union, the national *sindicatos*, or syndicates. The 26 national *sindicatos* of Spain are controlled by a bureaucracy appointed by a single chief (usually with cabinet status) who is himself appointed by the head of state. The principle of the *sindicatos* is that questions affecting labor should be dealt with by a tripartite organization of workers, employers and the state. The management side of industry is denied the right to fire employees or to pay them less than a minimum wage. Originally all employees were forbidden to strike. But in the face of repeated walkouts by Asturian coal miners from 1962 onward, and perhaps with an eye to world opinion at a time when Spain hoped for admission to the Common Market, the regime in 1965 decreed that labor thereafter would enjoy the right to strike. However, most labor disputes have been settled short of any work stoppage by a joint meeting of two representatives of employers and two of employees. The *sindicatos* cannot be called mere window dressing because they have gained for the workers substantial wage increases and social security benefits. Workers have been increasingly reluctant to risk losing the rewards that come through obedient membership in the *sindicatos*. Furthermore, there are ordinarily no strike funds for the modern Spanish worker to rely upon—a factor to discourage independence.

The principle underlying the *sindicatos* has never seemed applicable to conditions in Andalusia and through much of the countryside of Spain, where many workers are either unemployed, except at harvest time, or are tenant farmers. Thus the *sindicatos* are really only effective in the cities and in industry and mining. Ever since the radical economic stabilization plan went into effect in 1959, employers have been arguing that they cannot raise efficiency unless they can dismiss labor. But the regime in this instance has not yielded. If the *sindicatos* should fail, the whole basis for the regime would be endangered.

THE Roman Catholic Church is regarded as a strong support of the Franco regime, but this view can be an oversimplification. The relations between the Church and the government are regulated by the concordat of 1953, by which it was agreed that appointments of bishops and archbishops are made by agreement between the chief of state—Franco—and the Vatican. The Church has dominant influence over education, radio and television. Roman Catholicism is the "religion of state," and all other religions are officially referred to as "cults" and may be carried on only in private. Members of the Catholic clergy and religious orders are exempt from military service and are also exempt, in effect, from ordinary courts. Salaries and subsidies received by the clergy from the state are tax-exempt. In short, as a survey by the Princeton Center of International Studies sums it up in *Church and State in Franco Spain:* even the hierarchy recognizes that "the church in Spain never (or at least for several centuries) had it so good as under Franco."

WHAT is the strength of Roman Catholicism in Spain today? In 1966 there were 19,692 parish churches, 25,271 parish priests, 23,832 monks and 79,171 nuns. Church properties included 1,512 monasteries and 5,690 convents. A 1957 survey by an unofficial Christian trade union among 15,000 workers showed that 90 per cent of the workers were anticlerical and 41 per cent antireligious. Perhaps these figures are exaggerated. But it may well be that less than half of the people are to be regarded as faithful members of the Church. It is also true that however anticlerical many middle-class Spaniards may be, their wives are not.

One important body for spreading Catholic influence to leaders of public opinion has been the Opus Dei, an organization which grew out of student discussions in the late 1920s. Its original aim was to fight materialism, indifference and, through contacts with the intellectual elite, to work out a harmonious relationship between modern scientific advance and Catholic dogma. The organization has been authorized by the Pope and is active in more than 60 countries.

In Spain, it leans toward a strong support of capitalism operating under an authoritarian monarchy. It seeks to win over writers, journalists, university professors and top businessmen. The vows taken are chastity, poverty and obedience. They are personal vows, revocable at will, and the order has no insignia or uniform. The aim of the order can be regarded as simply to influence institutions and men discreetly toward an active Catholic interest.

In fact, it is a strong force supporting the Franco regime. (Catholic forces that are less than ardent backers of the regime are discussed in Chapter 7.) A key distribution point for Opus propaganda is the Estudio General de Navarra at Pamplona, a higher educational center of undoubted merit and originality which has attained university status despite bitter opposition by the University of Madrid. The financial resources of the Opus are reputedly huge—mainly from contributions by the rich members, who are expected to give the Opus all their income after paying their minimum living expenses. The men of Opus Dei control the Banco Popular, a number of magazines and several newspapers, including *Alcázar* in Madrid. For a time secrecy surrounded the question of who did or did not belong to Opus, but this is no longer true. Several key members of the Franco regime, men of great influence in state affairs, are known to be Opus members.

FINALLY, Spanish business must rank as a leading force backing the Franco regime. The Spanish army itself is in business, not only as a contractor of goods and services but through the activities of individual officers. Since military pay is poor, Spanish army officers often keep busy at side lines. A captain in the army education office, for example, might run a printing shop on the side. Boards of directors of large corporations are loaded with senior colonels and generals who are also on active military duty. Thus it is obvious that the army's main interest, in case there should be any change in government, would be to make sure that control did not escape military hands.

In few countries is business quite so dominated by banking, and Spanish banking is itself dominated by a few banks, most of them based in the north of Spain. Over the last decade, business has invested heavily and successfully in the regime. The potent combination of armed forces, Church, Falange and big business assures Franco of a force that will strongly oppose any radical change in the present structure of the Spanish government.

At a recreation center provided by their official union, Madrid workers and their families enjoy the largest swimming pool in Europe.

Aging Despotism Gone Paternalistic

After a quarter century of unchallenged rule, Francisco Franco projects a much softened image to the outside world. The regime, long devoted to currying favor with the Church and the privileged classes, now provides elaborate welfare benefits for the man in the street. Spanish labor has been given the right to strike. Press censorship has ostensibly ended. The jails have been nearly emptied of political prisoners. There is even talk of permitting an opposition.

DOUBLE APPEAL to business and labor in recent years has given the Franco government a broader basis of support than ever before

ECONOMIC PLANNER, Cabinet Minister Laureano López Rodó won Franco's endorsement of a program to modernize the Spanish economy and promote new industrial development.

CHEERING WORKERS *(opposite)* salute General Franco at the 1962 opening of a government housing project that provides low-cost apartments for 40,000 people in a Madrid suburb.

LABOR BOSS José Solís Ruiz reads a tribute to the general. Chief of the Falange, Spain's only legal party, and also head of the labor syndicates, Solís has kept most workers content.

RELIGIOUS PROCESSION winds through Franco's underground crypt in the Valley of the Fallen, a shrine on which many political prisoners were forced to labor.

GRANITE GALLERY is 285 feet long and is lined with six ornate chapels. Hewn from the interior of a mountain, the crypt is longer than St. Peter's Church in Rome.

GIGANTIC CROSS soars above the Valley of the Fallen in memory of the dead of the Civil War. The cost of building the cross alone was roughly one million dollars.

A VAST MAUSOLEUM testifies to Franco's piety and may serve as his tomb

THE CHURCH, *pervading all life, manifests itself in fervent spectacles of faith*

HOODED PENITENTS line up barefoot on a Seville street to march through the city during Holy Week, part of a week-long series of hugely ornate religious observances.

FRENZIED WORSHIPERS *(opposite)* shout and sing while carrying a statue of the Virgin through fields near the town of Moguer in a spring ritual of celebration.

6

A Tardy Economic Awakening

THE year 1959 in Spain began an era of great economic change. For 20 years after the Civil War the nation had gone its own way, isolated from the rest of the world in financial and business practices as well as in everything else. Foreign investment was unwanted, and Franco was as openly anticapitalist as he was anticommunist. Archaic Spanish industries, monopolistic and inefficient, creaked along behind trade barriers that kept most foreign products out entirely and imposed rigid quotas and exorbitant tariffs on the rest. The regime fixed wages and prices, as well as raw materials allocations, and Spanish entrepreneurs stayed in

business only at the pleasure of Franco. As in Hitler's Germany, economics was expected to remain subservient to politics.

When a group of government planners of a generation grown to maturity since the Civil War and "European" in outlook persuaded Franco to join the Organization for European Economic Cooperation, to adopt a stabilization plan and to free the Spanish economy from many of its controls, they wrought something like a miracle in the effect upon Spanish industry. Unfortunately for Spain, no miracle has touched Spanish agriculture.

Visitors to Spain are deeply impressed by the

country's jagged sierras and wide, dry river beds that make starkly beautiful patterns in yellow and brown and black. But this dramatic rocky land is not well suited to farming. In a total of about 125 million acres, 9 per cent is uncultivable, 50 per cent is forest or pasture, and only 41 per cent is farmed.

SPANISH agriculture today employs about 38 per cent of the total active population —or 4.8 million people. The land produces most of Spain's own food, but in every year since 1959 substantial imports have been necessary. Wheat, olives, fruit trees and vines dominate the cultivated land; food and wines make up the only large group of Spanish exports— more than 50 per cent of the total.

The state of Spanish agriculture is improving, but slowly. Half of the cultivated land is devoted to wheat and other cereals; wheat cultivation is about 15 per cent better than in pre-Civil War times. Fruit, vegetables, legumes and the production of agricultural raw materials (tobacco, cotton and other fibers) for industrial use have shown important increases. Since the late 1950s the average family's meat consumption has increased by about one fourth.

The general index of farm production rose by 35 per cent during the decade from 1952 to 1962. But a recent exodus from the land— 200,000 farm workers left the fields for city jobs in 1964 alone—is causing apprehension among Spain's economic planners.

One of the chief causes of the poor agricultural situation is the inefficient character of Spanish landholding. First is the problem of fragmentation, second the problem of *latifundios,* or large estates. On many of the smaller farms, especially in the north, the northwest and the central plains, the land is divided into small strips. In the province of Soria, for example, the average number of such strips to a farm is as high as 84. According to a 1953 agricultural census, there were 45.7 million such land parcels in the country, and about 90 per cent of them contained two and a half acres or less. Some of the farms were divided into

100 to 500 parcels, and their owners never found time to visit all of them.

An American sociologist has unearthed one case in the province of La Coruña in which a tract of land measured 38.3 square yards, but boasted three owners—one of them possessing the land, another holding title to the walnut tree that grew on it and the third having the right to collect six eggs a year from the property. Fragmentation of this kind is sometimes believed to foster community spirit. In practice, it leads to incessant wrangles over boundaries, pathways, access rights and water rights, prevents any adequate combination of farming and stock raising, and hinders mechanization or scientific agriculture.

Such is the general picture of agriculture throughout much of Castile, Aragon and the north of Spain. In the southern and western parts of the country another extreme hampers the development of farming. The most typical unit in this area is the *latifundio*. Some of these large estates have remained much the same in character since the days of the Roman Empire. The theoretical advantages of bigness—opportunity for mechanization and scientific farming on a large scale—have been wasted under this system. The *latifundio* has an absentee landlord who visits his estate annually at most, as if he were inspecting a remote colony. The landlord's agent is more interested in collecting rents than in encouraging production, and he is therefore likely to allow vast acreage to remain uncultivated.

THE huge agrarian working class is made up of tenant farmers and landless laborers. A large proportion of these people are unemployed except at harvest time, and most of the tenant farmers are inextricably involved with moneylenders. In Spain, only 13 per cent of the proprietors own about 65 per cent of the land. The big landowners (with 250 acres or more) are only 1 per cent of the proprietors but have 32 per cent of the cultivable land.

In Catalonia, along the slopes of the Pyrenees and in the eastern provinces along the

Mediterranean, there are fewer agricultural problems, because these areas have neither a great many *latifundios* nor much fragmentation. In general, tenants and owners working on this comparatively productive land can get off-season employment in local industries. Most of the fresh fruit and vegetables consumed by such great cities as Madrid, Barcelona and Seville come from these areas.

THE present regime has increased rice cultivation in Valencia, Aragon and Andalusia and has built up a cotton-growing industry. Since 1953 the development of irrigation has progressed. Efforts have been made to promote the wider use of farm machinery, to reforest the land and promote soil conservation, and to encourage the voluntary consolidation of small landholdings. The National Colonization Institute was set up in 1939 to tackle the problems of irrigation and the resettlement of farmers, to create local industries for the processing of crops, to develop local transport and to encourage scientific farming. The institute has launched development projects, notably in Aragon and Navarre, in Jaén and in Badajoz.

The Badajoz plan is typical of the institute's projects: it aims to revolutionize farming in this previously poverty-stricken province. In the area where the plan operates, large estates were either bought from the former owners or expropriated. The Guadiana River has already been partially harnessed to provide canals and irrigation ditches in a large area; land has been bought and resettled with farms averaging 14 acres in size; 36 new villages have been created. Altogether in Spain, some 1,650,000 acres have been irrigated since 1939; a total of 3,350,000 acres had previously been irrigated.

Under the Badajoz plan some of the new landowners live in houses on their new plots, but most of them are quartered in new *pueblos*. The 14-acre average is the calculated amount on which one man with some assistance (probably from his family) can farm and earn a living. On farms of more than 30 acres, the new farmer must reserve a certain percentage of land for

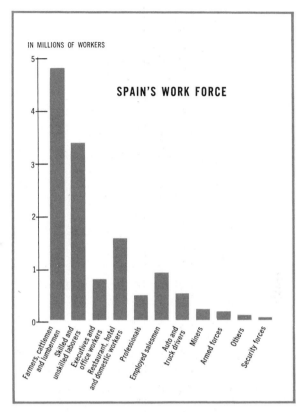

IN MILLIONS OF WORKERS

SPAIN'S WORK FORCE

(bar chart with categories: Farmers, cattlemen and lumbermen; Skilled and unskilled laborers; Executives and office workers; Restaurant, hotel and domestic workers; Professionals; Employed salesmen; Auto and truck drivers; Miners; Armed forces; Others; Security forces)

CONCENTRATION of labor on Spanish farms is reflected in this chart, which shows that people working the land constitute more than a third of the total work force.

wheat or fodder crops for a number of years; thereafter he may specialize in his choice of crops if he wishes and is free to farm as he likes as long as he keeps his land productive.

He buys the land on mortgage from the institute, and not until he has paid off the mortgage can the land be increased in size; it can never be subdivided. A former landowner in the area is allowed to keep 300 acres, and a new farmer can acquire as much as 112 acres, depending on the land's fertility. The rest of the *latifundios* in the area are divided and paid for at the price of nonirrigated land.

The aim of Spain's agricultural program is to irrigate 150,000 more acres every year—depending on funds available. But the transforming of dry land into irrigated land costs about $533 an acre on the average—a vast sum. In fact, the price of government-subsidized staples such as wheat and cotton grown under the Badajoz plan is one fourth higher than world market prices. Projects like the Badajoz plan have obvious social benefits and are expected to pay off financially in 40 or 50 years. Spain thus has an agrarian problem of huge proportions. In the long run, the future of the country will be decided by the manner in which this problem is solved.

THE Franco government has concentrated its main efforts on the industrial side of the country's economy, and it is in the cities of Spain that the most dramatic evidence of expansion can be seen. The beginning of major change was signaled when the United States, seeking cold war allies, entered into the military bases agreement with Franco in 1953. Over the following eight years America poured $1.2 billion into his country, 31.8 per cent of·it in foodstuffs, 32.8 per cent in raw materials for Spanish factories and 35.4 per cent in new machinery.

Still, the only capital Franco really wanted was that which came from Spain's ancient power centers, the seven largest banks of the land, traditionally allied with the landowning aristocracy. He looked with deep suspicion on Spanish economists who had studied abroad and talked about the interdependence of the European economies. When his lifelong friend, the naval architect Juan Antonio Suanzes, came up with the idea for a governmental agency to stimulate industrial expansion without foreign aid, Franco bought the plan gladly.

The result is a curious hybrid organization called INI (Instituto Nacional de Industría) that is part private corporation and part government institution. Its overall purpose is to stimulate new production, and by the mid-1960s it controlled more than 70 firms, many of which it had created. It produced Spain's first modern motor car, the diminutive SEAT, and directed the operations of her airline, Iberia. It built ships and manufactured fertilizers.

One of the prize creations of INI has been ENSIDESA (Empresa Nacional Siderúrgica SA), Spain's largest steel works, which is usually called Avilés after the name of the town where

it is located. It was begun in 1950 with an initial capital of $167 million from INI. Avilés was intended as a remedy for the steel shortage, which was holding up the whole process of economic development, and for alleviating the country's balance of payments situation by reducing steel imports. Beginning production in 1956, the Avilés works reached their planned capacity of 700,000 tons by late 1959.

But the expansion of the steel industry has brought on certain difficulties. It has meant that there has been a greater demand than ever for high-grade coal imports; the increased costs have therefore been passed on to the consumer by way of high prices or to the taxpayer through subsidies to the steel industry.

In mining, the general picture is less rosy because the modest expansion of the last decade has to be measured against a general decline ever since the early years of the century. Iron ore exports today are only half what they were in 1913, when they headed the list of Spanish products sold abroad. In the early years of this century, Spain was the leading European producer of lead; but now, with its mines mostly worked out, Spain produces only a third of what it did in 1913. Pyrites, on the other hand, have doubled their 1913 production figures, and the mining of low-grade coal has trebled. In recent years Spain has become an important producer of uranium; with an annual output of 50 metric tons of uranium oxide, it stands sixth among all nations in this category.

THE achievements of the Franco regime show up best in the production of electricity. In both hydroelectric and thermal power, there has been a vast increase since the Civil War. In 1953 a 10-year plan for power development was inaugurated. Now Spain has more power dams than any other nation of Western Europe, and its underground pumping station at the Aldeadávila Dam on the Spanish-Portuguese border is the largest on the continent. Westinghouse is building a nuclear power plant in Guadalajara province, while another and larger nuclear plant will be erected in the north.

Thus many important works have been accomplished, or inspired, by INI; but at the same time INI is responsible for many of the economic evils that in 1959 brought Spain to the edge of national bankruptcy. It encouraged and perpetuated monopolies. It founded inefficient industries. In an effort to control imports, it helped establish a chaotic currency with some 500 different exchange rates for the peseta. One economist recalls, "I was working for the Ministry of Commerce at the time and even we couldn't figure the system out." INI came to represent the closed-door type of thinking that gave Spain the highest tariffs in Europe.

BUT its main trouble was that it did not work. Despite all the efforts to keep imports down, they doubled from 1953 to 1958 while exports stood still. The cost of living index rose from 100 to 140. The nation's reserves melted away until by the summer of 1959 Spain had $63 million in gold and hard currencies in its vaults against debts of $67 million. Franco was faced with a choice between seeking a foreign loan, which meant agreeing to cut government expenditures, stabilize the currency, and open up the country to foreign investors (and possibly discomfiting foreign ideas), or re-establishing wartime food and fuel rationing. He opted for the loan and got $400 million from the International Monetary Fund with the participation of American banks.

Why Franco did this is an intriguing question. He had passed serenely unmoved through worse crises before. A Madrid banker explains it by saying, "When you are sick you go to a doctor." But long before Spain's economy was really sick, Franco had been consulting with "doctors"; diplomats of pro-European outlook, young economists with university teaching backgrounds. He had found room in his Cabinet of elderly comrades of Civil War days for vigorous younger men with new ideas: the Europeanist Fernando María Castiella to be foreign secretary; an advocate of a free economy, Alberto Ullastres, to be Minister of Commerce; another, Mariano Navarro Rubio, to be Min-

ister of Finance; a third, Laureano López Rodó, to be Secretary of the Cabinet; and later a fourth, Gregorio López Bravo, to be Minister of Industry. These men soon were being talked about for the efficiency with which their ministries operated.

It was also widely noted that some of the new ministers were members of *Opus Dei*. This led to charges by supporters of the old policies —conservative churchmen, the older army officers, INI's bureaucracy and the private bankers —that a "white masonry" was at work worming its members into ever more important posts with the eventual aim of taking over the country when the Generalissimo dies. But anyway the new ministers retained the confidence of Franco, who has the only vote in Spain that really counts.

Their successes were startling. The stabilization plan (carried out by Ullastres, who has since become Franco's ambassador to the Common Market, and Navarro Rubio, later head of Spain's central bank) not only refilled the country's coffers with astonishing speed, but also, by loosening the controls on trade, set the whole industrial economy astir. It was as if Spain had awakened from a long sleep.

SUDDENLY Spanish factories were turning out gas stoves, electric refrigerators and washing machines, and a new idea—installment buying—was getting them into people's homes. Some 30 per cent of Spanish families bought television sets. Latex came to Barcelona to girdle Spanish girls. And in a country that had never attempted mass production of automobiles, cars were popping out of factories at a 165,000-a-year clip. Chrysler, in partnership with Spanish industrialist Eduardo Barreiros, is making Dodge Darts in Madrid, while Citroën, Renault, Alfa Romeo and Auto Union have all opened up in Spain to compete with the Spanish government's own INI-controlled SEAT (pronounced like Fiat, of which it is the Spanish version).

To continue the impetus brought by stabilization, Franco in 1961 called in a team of experts from the International Bank for Reconstruction and Development to study his government's economic policies. One of their suggestions was for a government agency for economic planning. López Rodó was named to head such an agency. He gathered a committee of hundreds of experts from government offices and set to work. The planners borrowed a leaf from Puerto Rico's successful Operation Bootstrap and another from Jean Monnet's four-year plans in France, and added several volumes of study reports about the Spanish economy compiled on their own.

THE core of their plan was the establishment of seven *polos* or poles of development in various parts of provincial Spain: Burgos, Huelva, La Coruña, Seville, Valladolid, Vigo and Saragossa. To industrialists willing to establish plants at any of these places, the government offered rebates of up to 95 per cent on taxes during the first five years, exemption from import duties on equipment, and attractive factory sites in areas which the government had bought up—plus new housing and other facilities for the workers who would come to the new factories.

Typical is Valladolid, a gray stone and red brick town of 158,000 people set where the Duero, Pisuerga and Esgueva rivers meet on the Castilian plateau. Known to the Eighth Century Moslems as Belad Walid (or Governor's Town), it was for centuries the favorite residence of the Castilian kings. Ferdinand and Isabella were married there in 1469, Columbus died there in 1506 and Cervantes probably wrote parts of *Don Quixote* there. But by 1963 Valladolid had become a dusty market town with a few light industries and the main repair shops of the state railroads. And not far away was La Madurra, Spain's most important electricity transmission center.

In just two years of López Rodó's first four-year plan, Valladolid was transformed. Some 70 companies moved into town, bringing an investment of $76 million and 8,200 jobs. Among them was a three-factory complex that manu-

factures Renault Fours and Eights, and Austin trucks. Soon Valladolid achieved the ultimate status symbol of the industrial age: the traffic jam.

Tourism played a major role in Spain's economic transition. A department of tourism under another of Franco's bright young men, Manuel Fraga Iribarne, flooded Europe with invitations to visit the country, stressing sun, sand and bargain prices. Some of Spain's old moralistic laws were relaxed so that soon bikinis appeared on beaches where only a few years before men were being arrested for not wearing bathing suit tops. The government modernized nine old castles and monasteries and added them to its network of 40 hostels and inns, while the Spanish airline, Iberia, bought 21 new jets to hustle the hard-currency customers from Europe and America to the Spanish playgrounds.

Hotel building boomed. In 1962 Marbella was a sunstruck fishing hamlet between Malaga and Gibraltar; two years later it had three luxury hotels, a golf club, two movie houses, scores of bars and a growing skyline of glassy apartment houses. In nearby Torremolinos the beach on a hot August noon may offer standing room only. By the end of 1967 Spain expects to have spent about half a billion dollars on new hotels, with the government putting up about one third of the money. And as a result the bullfight season, which for a century ended in October, now unofficially extends throughout the year on the mild south coast, and in any resort town there are likely to be as many tourists as Spaniards shouting their olés.

ALL told some 36 million tourists spent 3.5 billion in Spain in the five years following stabilization, and the annual rate of tourist spending has topped $1 billion in recent years. These are amazing figures to those who knew Spain only a short time ago.

In the six years after stabilization, Spain's gross national product increased 100 per cent, making it the fastest growing nation in Europe

—albeit one of those that had the farthest to go. In 1965 per capita income in Spain topped the $500 mark by which economists divide the poor from the rich nations of the world. This left Spanish income still behind that of Italy, and the figure is only a third the per capita income of neighboring France. (Furthermore, the average is weighted by high rates in Madrid, Barcelona and the Bilbao industrial area; per capita income of farmers hovers around $100 a year, and their purchasing power is falling.) Nevertheless, Spain had come a long way from its per capita income rate of only $300 in 1958.

THE outlook for Spain's economic future is filled with uncertainties. Prices have been edging up steadily (a 15 per cent rise in 1965), and the grim word "inflation" is being heard on many sides. Ullastres, one of the chief architects of Spain's economic expansion, has bluntly warned the country: "The goose that lays the golden egg is our economy which, if it is well administered, will give us automatically every year an improvement of six, seven or eight per cent in our standard of living. But I don't think we can expand our consumption by say 20 per cent without killing the goose."

Another source of worry is that despite record tourist receipts the balance of payments turned against Spain in the mid-1960s for the first time since stabilization. This partly reflects the new industry's ever-increasing need for imports of heavy machinery, petroleum, chemicals, iron, steel and copper. And it points up the deterioration of Spanish agriculture, which makes it necessary to use foreign exchange for massive food imports.

Closely allied to the worry over an unfavorable balance of payments is Spain's failure so far to gain an "associate" membership in the Common Market, such as Greece and Turkey enjoy. Spain sells 39 per cent of its exports and buys 36 per cent of its imports from Common Market countries. It badly wants an arrangement to insure that its citrus fruit, olive oil and other agricultural products will continue to be accepted in those countries. But Spain is being kept out of the Common Market by the Scandinavian and Benelux nations on ideological grounds (the people in those places still cannot stomach Franco) and by Italy, which would just like to capture all the European orange business.

A fourth source of worry is the heavy dependence Spain must place on tourist spending and on remittances from Spaniards working abroad (850,000 men and women in 1966). An economic downturn anywhere in Europe must be felt immediately in Spain. "Tourism," one economist said, "can be a fickle lady. It is dependent in part on the weather, in part on fashion and in part on the cold practicality of prices. You can't suggest that our present economic expansion is based wholly on tourism, but it could not exist without tourism either. Let us hope therefore that there is no break in the weather."

A final worry is the slowness with which foreign investors have been attracted to Spain. While there has been some increase, the amount of foreign investment is not highly significant as yet. One reason for this, development planners think, is that the new and freer ground rules for capital have not been sufficiently advertised. Another reason was suggested by the Madrid economist who said: "Spain's image, until now, has not been secure. For years people abroad have been fighting the Civil War, although here in Spain we shudder at the very thought of it."

EVEN now, Spain's image is not altogether secure. Many observers feel that Franco's death could bring a return of violence to a country in which the art of representative government has been forgotten and where there is no machinery for an orderly transfer of power. The regime undoubtedly intends to press ahead vigorously with its industrial planning. But continued economic advance may depend ultimately on political advance. Spain must convince the world that the nation's future, after Franco goes, is one of stability and peace.

For a Backward Nation, a New Look

In the mind's eye of the average tourist, Spain is a land of ancient castles and picturesque villages and sun-drenched country landscapes perfect for framing in color slides. But novel landscapes have appeared in many parts of Spain, vistas that include factory buildings, electric power lines, four-lane highways and all the other appurtenances of a modern industrialized society. These symbols of a new era are evidence of the business expansion brought about in part by tourist spending, in part by government measures taken in the 1960s to stimulate capital investment. The expansion has brought jobs and better living conditions to many who knew only the bleakest poverty before. If economic advance is accompanied by billboards and traffic congestion and the despoilment of some once-loved Iberian scenery, well, the sun still shines over it all, and Spanish cash registers are making a happy sound.

DON PEPE HOTEL at Marbella is one of hundreds of modern tourist facilities that have appeared suddenly along Spain's Riviera, the once-somnolent Costa del Sol.

ALDEADAVILA DAM *(opposite)*, finished in 1964 near the Portuguese border, feeds a national power grid to help meet the expanding electrical needs of Spanish industry.

RADICAL CHANGE

has overtaken many parts

of the countryside where

government-provided

incentives have brought

swift industrialization

OUTSIDE SEVILLE, one of the cities named by state planners as "poles" of economic development, new factories and modern housing projects mushroom across farmlands that once provided pasturage for sheep. A wide variety of business ventures, financed by both domestic and foreign capital, has been attracted to areas of surplus manpower by offers of convenient plant sites, a five-year tax holiday, easy credit facilities and the duty-free importation of industrial equipment.

NEW INDUSTRIES in the booming cities bring a rise in employment and higher living standards for millions

FACTORY CENTER in the east, the city of Barcelona *(opposite)* stretches back from a busy waterfront to plants making automobiles and television sets. Cities like this draw many workers from impoverished farm areas.

ASSEMBLY LINE for Dodge Darts is part of a big automotive complex near Madrid. British, French and U.S. cars, as well as Spanish models, are now built in a country where not a single automobile was produced until 1950.

7

The Currents of Opposition

THE Franco regime has created a political vacuum. In Spain today it is not only unprofitable but dangerous to be too much concerned about politics. The new middle class appears to be devoting most of its energies to getting married young, making just enough money to live on and, if all goes well, buying a tiny car. To be sure, it is possible that the current vacuum of public opinion might be suddenly filled with some new, dramatic political idea. But the idea has not been forthcoming. Any sizing up of the opposition to the Franco regime can, therefore, be only speculative. No doubt there is a great reservoir of public resentment against Franco and a long-nurtured desire for revenge. In many cities of the south, for example, there are buildings that evoke bitter memories. In these buildings, which many inhabitants of the city have to go by every day, fathers and older brothers were shot during the Civil War. But as time passes, memories fade. Men now in their forties were adolescents at the end of the Civil War. A third of the population of Spain today was not even alive while the war was still in progress.

Is there then an effective opposition to the Franco regime? According to Dionisio Ridruejo, a disaffected Falangist who was at one time

97

The Currents of Opposition

Spain's national propaganda chief, the dissenters add up to a majority of the Spanish people —"those who got the worst of the bargain." Ridruejo believes that the potential opposition includes: "the middle class, the intellectuals, the working class, landless farm hands, and those who have suffered from discrimination and still feel the burden of the defeat. In addition there is a small group of the disillusioned and the conscience-stricken. They include liberal monarchists who consider Franco a usurper; *Falangistas* (members of the Falange), who, initially imbued with a revolutionary zeal for social renovation, now realize that they were made the pawns of a conservative cause; and some sincere Catholics, reluctant to see the Church yoked to the wagon of a violent and corrupt temporal power." But since the opposition is not organized, its potential strength can only be guessed at.

THERE are the monarchists, but it is difficult to regard them as either a single party or an out-and-out opposition group. The monarchists agree only on the desirability of restoring the monarchy, not on what kind of monarchy it should be or on how much voice the prospective monarch should have in the government. By the Law of 1947, Spain is technically a monarchy, although the present head of state, General Franco, has reserved for himself the right to name the king at such time as he sees fit.

The leading pretender to the throne is Juan, third son and heir (his two older brothers renounced the crown) of King Alfonso XIII. Don Juan was born in 1913. He is jovial, easily approachable and a tireless yachtsman. He apparently leans toward the idea of a constitutional monarchy, perhaps because of his background —an English mother, English governesses and three years with the British navy. But it is possible that he conceives of the Spanish monarchy as playing a far more positive role than the monarchy plays in Britain. Remarks made by Don Juan himself and by his closest supporters suggest that they think of the Spanish king's role as being on a lofty level equivalent to that

played by France's President Charles de Gaulle or the President of the United States.

Don Juan lives in exile in Estoril, Portugal. He is well off rather than very rich. Wealthy monarchists inside Spain, according to rumor, contribute to his support. His yacht, *Saltillo*, is not his own but is on indefinite loan from a friend of his father. Don Juan is advised by a 62-member privy council consisting of monarchists of various political opinions stretching from extreme rightist to constitutionalist. He has as secretaries a retired army major and a retired foreign service officer.

THE council meets from time to time in Estoril, but most of its members live in Madrid. A nine-member permanent committee meets in Madrid and acts as a kind of executive body for the monarchists in Spain. Don Juan shies away from declarations of policy, partly because of his carefully maintained attitude that the king should remain outside politics and partly because of a reluctance to commit himself in advance on debatable issues. He believes that his duty is to keep himself well-informed, to maintain contacts inside Spain and throughout the world, and to educate his children properly. He is visited continuously in Estoril by monarchist pilgrims.

It is difficult to assess Spanish monarchist strength with any precision. There is certainly no particular enthusiasm for the crown among the working classes. But to many thoughtful middle-class people, a constitutional king does seem a way out of the present dilemma—which appears to offer either prolonged military rule or a new time of chaos. There is only one organized monarchist group in the country, the Unión Española; its membership is small and its politics moderate, reflecting the views of intellectuals and professional people who would probably be considered enlightened conservatives in other countries. The Unión Española hopes to bring about a peaceful change of regime, seeks to put more urgency into Don Juan's bid for the throne and tries to convince him that a limited monarchy—along liberal rather than reactionary lines—is his best bet.

There is undoubtedly monarchist sentiment in the Church. Probably the Vatican and certainly a part of the Spanish hierarchy would welcome a constitutional king. The rich, influential religious organization, Opus Dei (*Chapter 5*), is well represented in Don Juan's privy council. Most army officers are also monarchist, but they, along with members of Opus Dei, are undoubtedly thinking of something much tougher and more regimented than whatever Unión Española has in mind.

There are several possible alternatives to Don Juan among the Pretender's many relatives of royal blood. But the obvious next choice is Don Juan Carlos, his eldest son. Juan Carlos appears to be a conventional young man without any special qualities distinguishing him from others of his class and set, except that he is fondly attached to his family and has already developed a strong sense of duty.

It is widely believed in Spain that Franco himself prefers the presumably more pliable son to his tougher-minded, Anglophile father. Certainly the general has shown Juan Carlos some apparent affection, mixed with deference. While the prince was studying at the University of Madrid, he was allowed to live in the Zarzuela Palace, a much more elegant house than his father's establishment in Estoril. In 1962 when the prince married Princess Sophia of Greece in Athens, Franco permitted representatives of the royal learned societies to attend the wedding in their official capacity, and he also sent the Spanish cruiser *Canarias* to Athens, accompanied by the Minister of the Navy.

THERE have been moments, in fact, when it had seemed that the father was deliberately being snubbed by the Franco regime. In the Spanish newsreel films of Juan Carlos' wedding, for example, Don Juan was shown playing a distinctly minor role in the proceedings. But Don Juan's own behavior has been more discreet recently than it was a few years ago. He has seemed to go out of his way to rebut suggestions that he is against Franco.

Whatever the official attitude toward Don Juan, monarchists feel that there is no question about who should succeed. If there is a restoration, the ruler must be Don Juan. In public and in private, Juan Carlos has insisted that he could never be king before his father. "I will do whatever Papa tells me," he has said. "I will never accept the crown during his lifetime."

ANOTHER group that might be classed as opposition is made up of the Christian Democrats. There are several factions bearing this political label, ranging from the moderate right to the moderate left, but all sharing a belief in some sort of representative government. Some Christian Democrats have been exiled for outspoken criticism of the Franco regime. Others have chosen to work within the regime and try to influence events in the direction of liberalization. An outstanding example of the latter is Joaquín Ruiz Jiménez, a law professor at the University of Madrid and editor of Spain's most serious and articulate Catholic review, who has served variously as Franco's Ambassador to the Vatican, as Minister of Education, and as a deputy to the *Cortes*, Franco's rubber-stamp parliament. Jiménez sees the best hope for Spain in the existence some day of a Catholic political party. He is considered by many as a potential Demo-Christian prime minister after Franco goes.

The Christian Democrats are Catholics, but their political activity is controlled by neither the Vatican nor the Spanish hierarchy. The group definitely seeks a peaceful change of regime. Because political activity by any party other than the Falange is illegal in Spain, Christian Democratic membership is impossible to estimate, but surely it constitutes one of Spain's two largest political bodies (the other is made up of Socialists).

Since the Catholic Church is so closely allied to the Franco regime, the Church cannot be listed among Franco's opponents. And yet the Church, through an organization called Catholic Action, has pressed hard for a relaxation of the regime's restrictions on freedom of speech and on labor activities. Angel Cardinal Herrera of Málaga, the enigmatic leading spirit of Catholic Action, detests the word "liberal" because of its anticlerical connotations in Spain, but he has campaigned vigorously for "social justice."

The right to strike, for instance, has been supported by the Catholic Action periodical *Ecclesia,* and by some members of the hierarchy. Better labor conditions and more freedom for workers have long been advocated by what amounts to a Catholic labor union, HOAC (Hermandades Obreras de Acción Católica), an offshoot of Catholic Action. HOAC has about 30,000 working-class members distributed throughout Spain, mostly in the towns. Their specific aim is to offer a Christian organization as a rival to the government-controlled labor unions. Individual members of HOAC backed the strikes in 1962 and onward (although the organization disclaims any strike role). The government has harassed HOAC members on occasion, and the group's publication, *Boletín,* has to be privately circulated.

THE liberals—inside and outside of Spain— might be classed as an opposition group, although obviously they must overlap into other groups already mentioned. The essential character of this group of opponents of the regime is that it is predominantly middle class—university and professional men and progressive businessmen. Their political creed may be described simply as a desire to draw Spain closer to the democratic traditions of western Europe.

They do not constitute a big organized body, but liberals exert an influence out of all proportion to their numbers, because many of them are men of international reputations in the fields of art and scholarship. A steady and conciliatory voice of the liberal opposition has been the writer and historian Salvador de Madariaga, now teaching at Oxford, who for many years spoke regularly to Spain by radio from France.

Separatist opposition to the strongly centralized Franco government is no longer a serious political threat. The Catalan movement now seems more a literary than an economic one, although it is still vocal: many riots have taken place in recent years over the right to teach the Catalan language in schools. But a hard economic fact is involved. Catalan businessmen increasingly regard the rest of Spain as a profitable market and also as a source of raw materials (the development of cotton in Andalusia and Estremadura is an example). But it is still true that hard-working, commercially minded Catalonia provides a sizable portion of the national income and feels that it should get a bigger share of government spending.

THE Basques continue to make up a remarkably self-sufficient and attractive community, holding to their Catholic integrity and their sense of social justice. In any discussion of the opposition, the Basques must be reckoned with because of their effective links with Spanish exiles—by way of the towns of St.-Jean-de-Luz and Biarritz nearby in France where many opponents of the regime make their headquarters. An émigré provincial government is maintained by a group of Basques in Paris.

The Basque Provinces are still the most devout region in Spain, with a higher church attendance than anywhere else. In 1960 nearly 350 Basque priests voiced open opposition to the Franco regime by signing a circular letter protesting government censorship and the use of torture by the police. In early 1962, Basque regional opposition to Franco, combined with Socialist agitation, spurred working-class unrest to such a degree that Bilbao, the tough industrial capital of the area, was second only to Asturias in strike activity.

It is impossible to pinpoint the political affiliations, if any, of Spain's 8.5 million laborers, but it is certain that the anarchists, who used to be strong in Barcelona and Andalusia, are still to be reckoned with.

The Socialists might be able to command the largest political force in Spain, but they are split by an internal battle between the exiles in command and the new generation inside Spain. The exiles who have enough freedom of movement to sustain their claim to leadership are growing old. One of the standard disputes among the Socialists revolves around the question of whether they should collaborate with the monarchists and the Communists. Many of the more politically aware young people opposed to Franco, especially the university students, are undoubtedly Socialist.

The Communists are the most effective opposition party today inside Spain. Their active membership is obviously small, and a minority of the leaders is of middle-class origin. But some of the leaders are strategically well-placed inside the *sindicatos* and are spread systematically throughout the universities. The party can also count on many Communist sympathizers who are not actually party members. The Communists have the advantage of a powerful radio station operating from Prague. It is called Radio España Independiente, but it also goes by the name of Radio Pyrenees to make its listeners believe that it is actually within sight of Spain. It broadcasts for seven hours every day on three separate wave bands and provides surprisingly accurate news bulletins, proving that reporters in Madrid can be in almost instantaneous touch with Prague. The trick is probably brought off by short-wave radio. The Communist broadcasts are enormously popular in Spain because they play up local sex and crime stories which do not appear in Spanish newspapers. They also stress an anti-American line with sly, continual references to Spain's "army of occupation."

ALL these scattered groups, officially banned, might seem hardly worth the name of even a potential opposition. But the fact is that they have behind them a latent force whose strength is unknown but which could be enormous—a people who want freedom. In part this force derives from the age-old opposition and distrust many Spaniards feel toward any central authority, especially toward a regime so centralized as that of General Franco.

When propagandists of the present regime lump all their opponents together as "anti-España," they imply that any opposition threatens to destroy the guardians of national unity and order. Spaniards are not greatly disturbed by the jingoistic taunt of "anti-España." Agents of government, except for local mayors, are invariably men from outside the *pueblo* in which they serve. Thus, the tax inspector in any town is likely to be considered the representative of an invading army sent from Madrid.

For people in small, remote villages of Spain, the state has often appeared as an enemy. The present regime has wooed many Spaniards away from this old-fashioned notion by providing such benefits as new schools and hospitals, credit for farmers and a form of social security. But in some rural areas the anti-Madrid feeling lingers on. For the average small farmer, the state is the tax collector who checks up on whether such and such a pig has produced such and such an amount of sausage.

THE essential point is that the *pueblo* and the poorer classes think of the rich and the representatives of any government as belonging to an entirely different world. And it is not a world that they greatly envy. Anarchists during the Civil War did not covet the riches of the bourgeoisie; they merely wished to destroy those riches as unclean.

Exiles speak hopefully today of potent new alliances and a growing ferment of opposition. But when it is all added up, tangible opposition to the Franco regime seems comparatively weak. Franco's support is formidable *(Chapter 5)*. The Strong Man himself recently complained: "In spite of all that has been achieved, I find that I encounter too frequently, in my governmental work and my visits and tours of inspection throughout the Spanish geography, a lack . . . of a true social conscience."

Franco may have been referring to the self-seeking of the privileged classes. But his words might also apply to whatever latent opposition exists. No combination of forces appears to have the unity of purpose or the resolve to agree on either a method of transition or the form of government that should replace the one now being administered from Madrid.

Disturbing Problems in a Modern World

Not all Spaniards have benefited from the nation's economic advance of recent years. Prosperity has come to a number of cities, where there is a growing middle class. But Spanish agriculture stagnates. Absentee landlords own giant estates, which they often neglect, while millions of impoverished peasants work tiny holdings with antiquated equipment. Most industrial workers are happy just to have jobs and social security, while the government dictates wages. But a troublesome minority aspires to more of an independent role for labor. Repeated strikes by coal miners have jolted the regime, which has also felt the sting of defiance from university students rioting to gain freedom from dictatorial controls. Especially disconcerting to Franco is the fact that many Spanish priests have joined miners and students in demonstrating for basic human liberties.

THICK FOREST of television antennas sprouts above the rooftops of Badajoz, bringing visions of a better life.

ANCIENT METHOD of threshing wheat is used by farm women who ride flat sleds drawn by horses and oxen.

TICKET BOOTH for the bullfights in Seville *(above)* attracts passersby as well as customers. Here and in the cafés the talk is frequently not of bulls but of politics.

MAGAZINE VENDOR in Madrid *(below)* offers nothing but bland reading matter. Censorship is easing officially, but no regular publication dares to criticize the regime.

SERIOUS STUDENTS at the University of Barcelona engage in a "bull session." Here and at Madrid University, students have clashed often with Franco's police over the issue of freedom to choose their own representatives in the campus unions run by the government. Such rioting led to the closing of the Barcelona school in 1966.

105

LABOR, though docile in the main, includes elements touched by world forces of progressivism and sometimes rebellious about the edicts of the state

A YOUNG PRIEST chats with miners in an Asturian town. Though the Church hierarchy normally supports Franco, liberal priests have often sided with striking workers.

YOUNG SPANISH LABORERS arrive by bus in Cologne, Germany. In the early 1960s, some 200,000 migrated each year to well-paying jobs in West Germany, France and the Benelux countries. The 30 per cent who return to Spain bring new skills and sometimes disturbing new concepts of free unionism as practiced under democracy.

WAITING for a new era, royal pretenders and opposition leaders eye the current regime

CHRISTIAN DEMOCRAT Joaquín Ruiz Jiménez, ex-envoy to the Vatican, is a leader among liberal Catholics who may have a future political role.

PRETENDERS to the throne *(right)* include Don Juan and his son Juan Carlos. Monarchists favor Don Juan, but Franco evidently prefers Juan Carlos.

COMMUNIST Dolores Ibarruri, known as *La Pasionaria* for her stirring Civil War speeches, influences Spanish Communists from exile in Russia.

LIBERAL Dionisio Ridruejo, once a Falangist, now hopes for some form of democratic government. He has been arrested by Franco several times.

8

City Street and Town Square

WHETHER he lives in the city, in a village or on a farm, the Spaniard works, eats, makes love, raises his children and spends his leisure hours in a manner that often seems as severely and gracefully stylized as the musical passages of a flamenco song.

City living in Spain, however, has elements that make it similar to city life in other countries. Modern industrial civilization is responsible for making every town in Europe look more and more like every other town, but standardization has not yet completely changed Spain. Nonetheless, rapid changes are on the way. Some sections of Madrid and Barcelona,

the two biggest cities, could be mistaken for sections of Paris or London, with the same blaring traffic, the same shiny new buildings going up, sidewalks full of smartly dressed people and the store windows glittering with luxury goods.

In Salamanca, Granada, Toledo and other provincial towns, life moves at a more sedate pace. Gothic churches and narrow streets left over from Moorish times still remind the visitor of Spain's vivid, violent past. Just outside the smaller cities, rural life often takes over abruptly: suddenly women can be heard singing as they gather to wash clothes along the riverbanks, just as they did in the Middle Ages.

In the cities, white-collar workers are much like office workers anywhere else. Legend says that a Spaniard is lazy. The truth is, he works hard at his job. When the modern Spanish office worker takes on a task that he considers worth doing at all, he attacks it in a furious spurt of energy, completes it to his own standards of satisfaction—and then sits back to rest before taking on a totally new task. The verb *descansar* (to rest) is one of the best-worn words in the Spanish language.

THE Spaniard is rarely interested in feverish activity for its own sake, nor does he particularly admire the go-getter or the man who strives to get rich quick. Much more admirable, by and large, is the person who manages to get along happily and with dignity on very little. "Making good" in a career is not half as important as job security and the prospect of a pension (a job with the government or with a large corporation is considered ideal). All the same, many Spaniards have to take on spare-time chores to make ends meet.

The usual city office hours are from 9 to 2:30 and then from 5 to 7:30. Most office workers go home to lunch and usually drop by a café to *descansar* before going back to work. Because of the hot climate, the siesta, if it can be worked in around 2 p.m., is a reasonable custom. Shops close at about 1:30, reopen at 4:30 and remain open until 7:30. The Spaniard relishes the idea of a full, rich night life, and so he likes to dine late—perhaps at 10 or 10:30.

A naturally gregarious man who delights in the intricate art of conversation, the Spaniard spends much of his time in cafés. He is probably a chain smoker and rolls his own cigars or cigarettes from his favorite cheap tobacco. He is rarely a heavy drinker, even though wine is one of the country's best-known products and at almost any hour is plentiful and inexpensive.

The café, therefore, plays an important role in social, business and political life. At crowded tables, in a heady, mixed aroma of wine, coffee and tobacco, opinions and ideas that never get printed in Spain's censored newspapers are vehemently aired—with gestures.

At home, in the city apartment, heat and flies must be kept out, but the task of fighting moisture and cold is hardly worth the effort. In the south, the heating problem is solved with a charcoal burner, placed in the living room under a table around which the family gathers for both meals and conversation. The house in southern Spain is a two-story building enclosing a patio that is shaded by awnings and decorated with shrubbery, potted flowers and sometimes fountains.

At table, the average family does without—by necessity—but higher income caused by industrial expansion in the cities is bringing some improvement in dietary standards. The Spaniard now eats 61.6 pounds of meat a year (the average American eats more than 207 pounds, and the average Englishman about 156 pounds). The average Spaniard drinks about 100 quarts of milk a year (the American drinks 142 quarts, and the Briton 109 quarts).

Spanish food is not as varied or as daintily prepared as French or Italian cuisine, but it is substantial. Sea food—shrimps, prawns, crayfish and crabs—is plentiful throughout the country. In the north, fresh tuna steaks are cooked in a heavy tomato and onion sauce. In general, the dishes are not as highly seasoned as Mexican food, but garlic and peppers are lavishly used. A basic of the Spanish diet is *pulses*—dried beans, lentils and chick-peas—which are cooked in a variety of ways in different parts of the country, sometimes with boiled chicken, sometimes with boiled beef or boiled bacon or salt pork and sausage.

A COLD soup served with croutons, *gazpacho*, which used to be eaten by poor Andalusian peasants, has become popular all over Spain and even in America. To a base of oil and vinegar are added finely strained tomatoes, garlic, bread crumbs, chopped cucumber and onions. Madrid specializes in roast suckling pig, roast lamb and *paella*, a mixture of saffron rice, bits of assorted sea food and bits of meat and chicken, topped with thin slices of sweet red pimiento and green peas. Spaniards consume a great deal of beer, but sherry, for those who can afford it, is the favorite drink.

A VAST number of Spanish workers—including most of those in the countryside—earn less than enough for their basic needs. But wages in industry have greatly improved. The legal minimum for unskilled factory labor, which was 36 pesetas (60 cents) a day in 1962, became a dollar a day in 1966, and "fringe benefits" (meaning extra pay for "hard work," for example, and not social security, which is considered a right) can boost the laborer's take-home pay to $2.85. The skilled mechanic's legal pay rate is $1.11 to $1.20 a day, but fringes can raise it to a sum between $3.20 and $3.77.

Housing for workers is a major problem. A national housing plan begun in 1961, offering subsidies and easy credit to builders, has resulted in a substantial construction boom. But high-cost apartments and luxury accommodations for tourists have provided such dazzling profits to investors (a thousand per cent to many landowners on the Costa del Sol) that activity in the private sector has far outstripped the public effort to provide low-rent facilities for the poor. Large government housing projects have gone up in a number of urban areas, but the demand for space far exceeds the supply. In privately owned apartment buildings, rents have tripled since 1959.

Despite inflation, the standard of living in Spain has risen unmistakably during the last decade. The introduction of installment buying, combined with television advertising, has managed to get refrigerators, washing machines and many other modern conveniences into the homes of city dwellers. In 1965 there were more than 650,000 passenger cars in use and more than a million motorcycles.

In meeting other people, the Spaniard has always found that social status is of less importance than region. For the vast majority, the interest aroused by a stranger is not over the question of who he is so much as what part of the country he comes from. There is no difference in accent between people of different social standing from the same region, unless education has wiped out the rusticisms of the rich. Even the well-to-do of Andalusia, for instance, speak with local dialects and often exaggerate their speech difference when traveling "abroad" in Madrid or some other big city.

Within the big divisions of the country (Andalusia, Estremadura, etc.), there are differences of speech even from one *pueblo* to the next: in one, for example, the double "l" may be pronounced something like "j"; in another, a few miles away, it may be pronounced "y." There are also differences in the use of words and in customs: in one *pueblo* the accepted place for courtship is at the door, in another at the window. An assumed fierce rivalry toward one or more nearby towns is one of the strongest local passions.

There are, of course, class differences. In some ways, no country in western Europe has such a rigid class system, but often a man is not really interested in rising from one social stratum to a higher one. And yet Spaniards of all ages, sexes and classes like to aim their most derisive jokes at pompous pretense. It nevertheless follows that even the poorest man can take the most meticulous care about his grooming. A high polish on the shoes is a tradition passed down from the *caballero* (gentleman on horseback), whose shiny boots served notice that he rode his own horse and did not walk along dusty roads with lesser men.

O NE notable development of Spanish life during the last few decades has been a steadily increasing movement of population into the large towns. This trend began after World War II when the people of smaller towns made their way toward the capitals of provinces to get jobs in expanding industries. (The trend has been most noticeable in four areas: Barcelona, Bilbao, Madrid and Cordova-Seville.) The population shift has continued as young men have increasingly gone into the cities for work. The size of Madrid has boomed from about one million in 1935 to more than 2.6 million today. The shift of population to the cities has also brought people from different provinces together for the first time and thus indirectly contributed to the growth of a greater national consciousness.

BUT most of the Spanish people still live outside the big cities. The majority of Spaniards in the central and southern areas live in *pueblos*, the small towns and villages. Even farmers and farm laborers who go out every day to work on the land go back at night to their *pueblos*. (The small farmers of the northeastern provinces are exceptions; they usually live on their land.) The fact is, farmers in many parts of Spain have no particular love for—or even sense of duty toward—the land from which they wrest a living. Spanish literature in its bucolic passages is seldom softly sentimental. On the contrary, Spanish writers frequently give the impression that life on the farm means solitude, loneliness, hard times and failure.

The central fact of Spanish country life is poverty. And as if grinding poverty were not enough, the farmer is faced with continual insecurity. All harvests are uncertain, and the difference between a good harvest and a bad one is often the difference between barely getting by and real hardship.

Poverty and insecurity are powerful forces for the preservation of some of the old-fashioned rituals of living. Life in Spain revolves around the family. Birth control is forbidden by the Church, and the average family has at least two or three children; 10 or more are not rare (those who wish to limit their families generally employ the Church-countenanced "safe period").

Children are loved and fussed over with a complete absence of the emotional reserve that exists in many western societies. Parents who give their children a devoted upbringing can in turn expect to receive unquestioned love and attention in their old age. Much of a Spaniard's earnings is earmarked for the support of

his older relations. A man keeps in solicitous touch with all of his own family and his wife's, and is ready to help them in an emergency. In turn, he expects help from his relatives when he himself gets into trouble.

Sex has a forthright role in the whole scheme of Spanish society. A man, by definition, must be virile, fearless and ready at all times to put up a physical defense for his own honor and that of his family. If he loses his *hombría* (literally, manliness), he has earned the contempt of his fellow men. A woman must be feminine, a good homemaker and, above all, chaste. An unmarried girl who loses her virtue —or even risks her virtuous reputation—has small chance of finding a husband. In times past, a married woman who "dishonored" her husband could be put to death. Modern times have outlawed the death penalty for adultery, but the old traditions continue to discourage carefree love affairs. The popular fictional female of American movies, women's magazines and television, who believes that the world is "well lost for love" (or sexual desire), is baffling to a well-brought-up Spanish woman.

EDUCATION sets out to emphasize the difference between the sexes and to keep the sexes apart. Boys are brought up to emulate their fathers, and girls to imitate the social graces and household skills of their mothers. Boys and girls usually go to different schools, and education is compulsory until the age of 14. The sexes remain apart, if parents and public pressure can manage it, until the beginning of courtship, which usually starts between the ages of 15 and 18.

Courtship in past centuries, particularly in the south, was a fine, formal Spanish mixture of sentimentality and hard common sense. The details of the old rituals are gradually becoming blurred; but in both city parks and village squares, groups of boys and groups of girls, on a pleasant evening, still wander in opposite directions. A passionately intent look and a sigh, a provocative lowering of eyelashes or an exchange of demure smiles may be enough to insure a first meeting. Henceforward, the *novio* (suitor) may publicly make his plea for the hand of the *novia* (girl).

The courtship, which may go on for weeks, months or years, can be carried on at a window or at a door. In any case, the formal overtures take place in public, and any physical contact such as hand-holding or kissing is against the rules. A girl who encourages too many *novios* is at best flighty, at worst taking a chance on being considered unchaste. She thus risks a bad reputation and possible spinsterhood. During the courtship, the family of the girl goes to elaborate pains to take no notice that anything romantic is afoot.

When the two young people have talked things over to the point of agreeing to marry, the *novio* calls on the girl's father. His mother then calls on her mother. The formal dramatic script is played out to the end when the girl's father is finally persuaded by his wife to give his blessing to the union. As a matter of fact, the parents have very little voice in their children's choice.

The *novio* now gives some money to his *novia* to buy furniture for their house. There is much insistence on the new couple's living in its own separate house, regardless of the economic advantages of two or three families living together. A wedding day is fixed perhaps three or four months in the future.

AFTER the marriage, the new wife takes over control of the household and subsequently of the children. The husband may assume the role of a sort of favored eldest son, now happily living in a household in which he is the master. He is more or less free to look for sexual excitement and to demonstrate his virility outside his home—if he can afford it. He will undoubtedly have the feeling that he is sinning, but he will hope to make his peace with the Church in his old age.

The husband is able to control, but not to dispose of, all his wife's possessions. At his death, the law of inheritance in many parts of Spain provides that half of his estate goes to

his widow and half is to be divided among the children. The widow's portion at her death is also divided among the children.

Outside working hours, the Spaniard amuses himself with many things. Nearly one half of the money available for "culture and recreation" is spent on movies. The cinema is cheap except in large towns, and there are about 7,500 movie houses with enough seats for more than four million people. The attendance rate is high: in 1965 the average Spaniard went to the movies 14 times (in the United States, it was 12.4 times; in France, 8.2 times). In 1964, of the 288 full-length pictures shown, 43 were made in Spain, 97 in the United States.

LIFE in a Spanish *pueblo* might appear dull to an outsider, but in addition to the excitement of marriages, births and deaths, in which everyone is interested, there are countless *ferias* and *fiestas* in which everyone takes part. The nonreligious *feria* (fair) in the remoter country districts is an occasion for horse, cattle, and sheep trading. But the briskest business at these festivals is carried on by the people who sell sherry and cognac at only a few cents a glass. Usually the *feria* begins with a street parade which ends up at hastily decorated booths and tents set up on the outskirts of town. The annual *ferias* held in Seville and in Jerez de la Frontera are lavishly planned occasions that include bullfights, horse races, parades and dancing in the streets.

But as a rule, the religious *fiestas*, with the full cooperation of the local clergy, are better costumed and stage-managed. The elaborately carved *pasos* (religious images), mounted on wooden platforms, are carried through the streets, often to the accompaniment of rolling drums and wailing penitents. The carved figures surrounding the harshly realistic figure of the crucified Christ are clothed in brocades and velvets, and their jewels sparkle in the sun and glitter in the light of candles and torches.

The best-loved national sport is still bullfighting, which has been given a great boost by tourism. Many non-Spaniards feel that a visit to Spain is not complete without an after-noon spent at the *corrida*. Soccer, which drew overflow crowds in the 1950s, has lost attendance since the games have been televised. Television has also cut into the gate for bullfighting. After all, good seats at the bull ring are $8.50; at the soccer stadium $2.50; and almost every tavern in Spain has a TV screen.

Bullfighting is not so much a sport as a spectacle. It is a play in three acts (the *tercios*) with a definite plot. The plot specifies that the bull die. Bullfighting is also a kind of ballet, performed in highly stylized, traditional movements that require great skill and grace. But most important, bullfighting is an exhibition of manhood and courage. The brave man must not only master the bull: he must first master his own fear.

BULLFIGHTS are not continuous, year-round spectacles in Spain. From March to October, Sundays and Thursdays are bullfight days in Madrid and Barcelona; during the same months, Sunday is the day in Valencia. Many of these events are not real *corridas* (full bullfights), in which full-fledged matadors take part, but *novilladas*, where the bulls are young and the matadors are youths who have not yet been granted the *alternativa*—the accolade bestowed on those who have reached the top rank of *matadores de toros*.

In other parts of Spain, bullfights are staged only during the week when a town is having its *fiesta*. Once a year, at the time for celebrating the town's patron saint, there may be a bullfight every day. Sometimes a small town's festival is enlivened by amateur fights in which boys fight a bull in the main square.

Traditional folk songs and dances play an important part in the Spaniard's hours of recreation. The flamenco, the Andalusian dance that features passionately stamping heels and a rattle of castanets, seems to have become a gypsy monopoly, since the gypsies produce superior flamenco dancers and the best accompanying *cante hondo* singers. The guitar accompaniment to the dance has a sultry beat that is emphasized by the rhythmic clapping of hands. The song, which usually begins with one loud, sustained cry, invariably recalls the first cry of the Moslem imam from his high minaret, calling the faithful to prayer. Flamenco songs and dances are performed in all Spanish music halls and night clubs and at every Andalusian *fiesta* and *feria*.

READING, as a recreation, is not a national habit. In 1960, almost 13 per cent of the Spanish population was considered illiterate, and the average Spaniard spent only about a dollar a year on books. But books have become Spain's number one export among manufactured articles—the bulk of the shipments going to Latin America, where Spain is working in many ways to regain cultural influence.

Censorship results in such general ignorance of outside events that a high court judge in Madrid heard of Hitler's massacre of the Jews only at the time of the Eichmann trial in 1961. But since enactment of a new press law in 1966, Spanish newspapers have begun cautiously to report major happenings in the world.

There were an estimated 1,650,000 television receivers at the end of 1965 (there were about 4.5 million in France), and 4 million radio sets (against 10 million in France).

Meantime, with a million-peseta state subsidy, the theater is booming in Madrid. Six new theaters have opened their doors since 1962. A controversial political play, *La Camisa* (The Shirt), by a leading playwright, Lauro Olmo, described a group of unemployed workers living in a slum area. Their problem seemed to be a choice between winning the soccer lottery or having to leave Spain. At the Barcelona opening, four members of the audience shouted *Viva la Camisa!* (Long Live the Shirt!) and were promptly arrested. *Viva la Camisa!* has now become a symbol of working-class dignity.

The Spaniard works hard, and when the time comes for recreation, he plays just as hard. But whatever he does, he will do in his own good time, without being prodded or hurried. Push a Spaniard, and he comes to a dead standstill.

Carrying a tray of unbaked bread, a young girl kicks open the wooden door of the communal oven in the small village of Deleitosa.

The Simple, Hard Life of the Village

The village of Deleitosa in Estremadura is typical of the more backward parts of Spain. The lives of the people are dominated by the simple but brutal problem of growing enough to eat. When these classic pictures were taken by W. Eugene Smith in 1950, some signs of the 20th Century were present: flickering electricity, a few radios. Since then television has come to the village tavern. But in its essentials Deleitosa has changed little since medieval times.

SUN-BAKED HOUSES of stone, wood and clay, where families of six or eight may sleep in one room, face on Deleitosa's unpaved streets. Burros, dogs, chickens and pigs wander about in a friendly, informal fashion, giving the village a strong animal odor. In the background is the belfry of Deleitosa's 16th Century stone church.

HARDWORKING FARMER of Deleitosa *(above)* leans heavily on his flattened plow to scrape the dry soil back into shallow furrows where beans have been planted.

YOUNG PLOWBOY carries his primitive plow to the fields where he hires out to village farmers at a small daily wage. Boys begin working at a very early age.

MAKING HIS ROUNDS, the local physician, Dr. José Martín *(left)*, confers with a patient. Doctors can perform minor operations at a local dispensary.

SPINNING THREAD, a peasant woman *(opposite)* moistens fibers of locally grown flax as she winds them onto her polished, tapering spindles.

GOING TO CHURCH for First Communion, a seven-year-old, dressed in traditional white, looks pensive as she waits for her mother to lock the door.

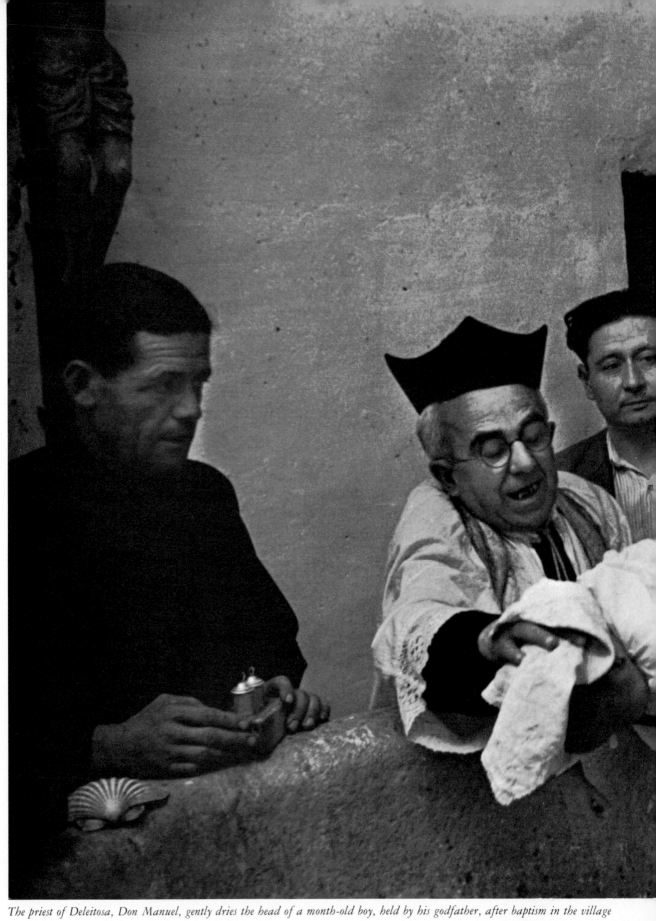

The priest of Deleitosa, Don Manuel, gently dries the head of a month-old boy, held by his godfather, after baptism in the village

church. Whether a villager is pious or not, the great events of his life, from birth to death, are formally celebrated in the church.

The Upward Reach of Art

SOON after American air bases were first established in Spain in the 1950s, people sitting at sidewalk tables on the streets of Segovia could look up and see B-47 jet bombers amazingly framed in the 2,000-year-old arches of the aqueduct. The B-47s are now obsolete. The 2,700-foot-long aqueduct, built by the Romans during their occupation of Spain and one of the country's early artistic landmarks, is still carrying water to Segovia.

In the early Christian centuries, the architecture of Spain was a vivid conglomeration of styles and influences. The Visigoths, who succeeded the Romans on the peninsula, used the horseshoe arch that was to become one of the hallmarks of Islamic construction in Spain. The Moors later contributed the flowing patterns, the luxuriant two-dimensional ornamentation and the multifoil arches so characteristic of the Spanish south.

The fusion of styles into what would eventually be regarded as typically Spanish began with the Moslem concept of architectural planning. In contrast to the western insistence on symmetry, the Moors fragmented space, divided it into compartments and shifted directional axes.

In 786 A.D. the Caliph Abdul Rahman began the construction of the Great Mosque of

Cordova. With all its additions, it took several hundred years to complete and is the biggest mosque west of Mecca. Moslem architects, building quickly and expediently, plundered old Roman structures for building materials. When the classical Roman columns were too short for the grand Moorish design, the Moors used them anyway and topped them with extra tall capitals. The mosque has 19 aisles and a multicolored forest of columns adjoining an open court. It covers 242,250 square feet, but surprisingly is only 30 feet high. During the reign of Charles I, a Christian cathedral was planted among the pillars, but the mosaics, fountains and beautiful tiers of Moslem arches make the mosque one of the great architectural legacies of the Moors to Spain.

ANOTHER one is the Alhambra at Granada. Sprawling and lacking in symmetry, languidly spilling down the hillside it rests on, the Alhambra appears to have no architectural unity in the conventional sense and from its exterior looks like any other medieval castle. It has no visual center of balance, and the eye of the visitor does not automatically follow a consistent course. It is unprepossessing and seems haphazard. But inside, it is certainly one of the most beautiful groups of buildings in the world—a breathtakingly subtle orchestration of light and shadow, pools and gardens, fountains and arcades, closed apartments and open courts with filigreed arches.

French influences affected Spanish architecture during the 11th and 12th Centuries when monks and priests from Cluny moved south to stimulate and reform Spain's religious life. This immigration influenced the building of a series of Romanesque churches. Some of them may still be seen along the pilgrimage route to the most impressive Romanesque structure on the Iberian Peninsula: the Cathedral of Santiago de Compostela in Galicia, the westernmost region of Spain. From all parts of the Christian world in times past, multitudes have journeyed to Santiago (St. James) to worship at the spot where the patron saint of Spain was

believed to have been laid to rest after his martyrdom in the Holy Land.

Before long the Romanesque in Spain gave way to the Gothic, also at first a French import. With the addition of local touches, a sort of native Spanish Gothic evolved. This period produced some of the finest cathedrals in the Christian world. The building or rebuilding of a cathedral was often begun soon after a city was reconquered from the Moslems, and the structures were usually more massive and more irregular in exterior shape than their prototypes in northern Europe. The outstanding examples of Spanish Gothic stand in Barcelona, León, Burgos, Toledo, Salamanca, Gerona and Seville.

Unlike the great French Gothic cathedrals that impress by sheer height, the Spanish cathedral has an exterior of unbroken rectangular massing. The cathedral at Seville, with its interior of pointed arches, lofty vaults and traceried stained glass windows, is one of the finest achievements of Gothic Europe.

LIKE Spanish architecture, Spanish literature is a braid of alien roots. Its development shows Arabic, Hebrew, Germanic, French and Italian influences. The first great work of Spanish literature was the *Poema de Mío Cid*, a 3,735-line epic poem written, probably around 1140, by an unknown author. The poem celebrates Spain's national hero, El Cid, who occupies in the heroic tradition of Spain the sort of place that King Arthur occupies in the tradition of England. But more is known of the Cid than of Arthur. He was an actual 11th Century warrior whose name was Rodrigo Díaz de Vivar. Full-bearded and virile, he was a soldier of fortune who became the first living symbol of Spanish nationalism. The Cid who emerges from the poem, like the actual prototype might well have been, was a loving husband and devoted father, deeply religious, ruthless but fair in battle, healthy of mind and strong of body. In short, a true Spaniard.

Quite another mainstream of Spanish literature began in the time of the great lyric poet

Juan Ruiz, a 14th Century priest who had a splendid sense of humor and a long series of scandalous love affairs. He confesses all in the *Book of Good Love.* Full of sly ironies, he dutifully extolls *buen amor* (love that comes from God). But since people are sinners and indulge in *loco amor* (carnal love), he feels obliged to include instructions about its practice.

In an easy, spontaneous verse that combined a variety of meters, Ruiz created character types that would recur throughout Spanish literature, notably the go-between in love affairs and the *pícaro* (vagabond). Like Geoffrey Chaucer in England, Juan Ruiz stood far above his contemporaries in the Middle Ages in Spain.

The last of the poets of the Spanish Middle Ages was a soldier who occasionally set verse to paper. Yet Jorge Manrique distilled into his poems a kind of mournful nostalgia that remains as an essential sentiment in the Spanish spirit.

Like many Spaniards, Manrique had a feeling of sadness over past glories. Even before the era of greatness *(Chapter 3)* he was dolefully recalling the

GREAT FIGURES of Spanish literature, romantic Don Quixote and practical Sancho Panza *(rear),* shown in this Daumier drawing, are said to represent the two poles of the Spanish temper.

great moments of Spanish history that had flared so intensely and departed so suddenly. In his *Coplas,* Manrique was mourning the death of his father, but his work stands within a stream of stoic melancholy that flows unceasingly in Spanish literature. He writes:

> *What became of the king, Don Juan?*
> *And the Infantes of Aragon,*
> *What became of them?*
> *What became of the gallants all?*
> *What became of the feats and deeds. . . .*

Early Spanish literature also included a work that had a powerful influence on later writers, Fernando de Rojas' *La Celestina,* published in 1499. An earthy story with an operatic plot, it concerns a retired prostitute who spends her time functioning as a witch, procuress and midwife. Its dialogue, psychological realism, picaresque passages and warm-blooded characterizations launched a great prose tradition.

In *Celestina,* for the first time in Spanish literature, a thematic collision takes place between idealism and naturalism, a recurring element in literary masterpieces yet to come. Similarly, such early Renaissance writers as San Juan de la Cruz (mystical lyricism) and Fray Luis de León (intellectual lyricism) helped prepare the language to receive its greatest master.

Men of letters must arrive on the scene at the proper moment. Just as Shakespeare was born in England at a time when political, linguistic and social confluences had set the stage for his genius, Don Miguel de Cervantes Saavedra was born near Madrid at a similar moment—1547—in Spanish history. His life would make a splendid Hollywood adventure film. The son of an impoverished apothecary surgeon, he was forced to find a career in the army. He lost the use of his left hand in the Battle of Lepanto, fought in Naples and Tunisia, and was on his way home when his galley was attacked by Barbary pirates. He was carried off to slavery in Algiers and, after bungling numerous escape attempts, was finally ransomed.

Having failed to win great distinction as a soldier, Cervantes also failed, for more than

20 years, to win critical acclaim in literature. At the age of 50, under the weight of discouragement—a threadbare old man who had been in jail for debt and was finally ready to accept his own mediocrity—he sat down to write an amusing short story and ended up producing the greatest masterpiece of Spanish literature.

All the ingredients for his work were at hand —the picaresque, the pastoral, the groundwork of literary realism, the national epic poem of the ideal—and Cervantes drew it all together in *Don Quixote de La Mancha,* a book that has been reprinted more often than any other volume except the Bible.

LIKE much that is great in Spanish literature, *Don Quixote* began as a burlesque. It set out to poke fun at the authors of all the endless stories that so exalted the codes of chivalry that no one could take them seriously. In the insanely idealistic knight-errant (Don Quixote) and his relentlessly practical and materialistic squire (Sancho Panza) Cervantes was describing the extremes that must be brought into balance in a healthy mind. His book thus became nothing less than the abstract and the chronicle of every human soul.

Cervantes' time was a prodigal one with literary genius. Among his contemporaries were the two greatest poetic dramatists of the Spanish tradition, Lope de Vega and Calderón de la Barca.

Félix Lope de Vega Carpio, author of such excellent plays as *Fuenteovejuna* and *El Mejor Alcalde el Rey* (The Supreme Judge, the King), wrote some 1,800 full-length plays, many of which were extremely well turned. He dashed off religious plays, historical plays, mythological plays, pastorals, court intrigues, comedies of manners, almost everything that was possible on a stage. He was probably the glibbest man who has ever lived, and he must have gone around telling his friends that he would like to get more writing done but he just could not find the time. He fought with the Spanish Armada, and perhaps he was the only Spaniard for whom the adventure was not a total loss. He whiled away his time on board ship by turning out 11,000 lines of verse, which he later published as an epic poem called *La Hermosura de Angélica.*

Apart from sheer volume, Lope de Vega's contribution to the Spanish drama was inestimable. He virtually created its tradition singlehanded and supplied the national theater with enough plots, situations, themes and characters to last a thousand years. His work, which does show the strain of hasty preparation and therefore contains no single towering masterpiece, is nevertheless much more than a warehouse full of potboilers. His poetry brought the spirit of his country into the theater in living form.

The year of Lope de Vega's death, another writer of distinction moved into the spotlight. A student of canon and civil law, Pedro Calderón de la Barca, was a disciple of Lope de Vega, who produced secular and religious plays that explored the Spanish character with much greater profundity than did the examples of the master. His *La Vida es Sueño* is a philosophical play about the unreality of life. His so-called honor tragedies clearly set forth the peculiar Spanish concept of *pundonor*—a rigid sense of personal and family honor once so strong in the Spanish mind that the smallest social blemish could start a chain of vengeance and bloodshed.

CERVANTES had a hard time getting started in his career, but other creative men in 16th Century Spain were more fortunate. One such talented man was a moderately wealthy painter whose name was Domenikos Theotokopoulos. In his Toledo neighborhood this artist was known as El Greco—The Greek.

The high point of painting in Spain came later than it did in literature, and El Greco was the first Spanish painter of lasting significance. He himself had an inkling of his true worth. Complaining about the pay he was getting for one commission, he wrote: "As surely as the rate of payment is below the value of my sublime work, so surely will my name go down to posterity . . . as one of the greatest geniuses of Spanish painting."

Born in Crete, he went to Venice and then to Rome when he was a youth. In Italy, he copied and learned from the works of the masters, particularly Titian, Tintoretto and Michelangelo. Migrating to Toledo about 1577, he painted a large canvas showing King Philip II kneeling in serene prayer amid an assortment of human and heavenly figures posed in heaven, purgatory and hell.

H E sent the painting off to Philip II and was immediately commissioned to do another one. But his figures were so disproportionately elongated and disturbingly unearthbound that the king ultimately rejected his work, and El Greco never became a court painter.

A dramatist in oil, he once crossed the Tagus River and sketched his city from the northeast. In reality, Toledo rises steeply from the river, a terraced warren of jumbled buildings, making no particular impression on the passing eye. But El Greco pinched one portion of the town until it soared to a pinnacle dominated by its cathedral and palace. The result was his celebrated *View of Toledo*. A portentous thunderstorm fills the air, and the city is illuminated by an unearthly light.

El Greco was preoccupied with a mystical aspiration to unite the materialistic earth with the spiritual life of heaven, and nearly everything he painted reaches upward like a Gothic spire. The *Burial of Count Orgaz*, his tremendous canvas that still hangs in the church of Santo Tomé, is a flowing unification of earthlings, saints and heavenly hosts. He made enough from his painting to live in luxury, but in later centuries his work was either ignored or despised.

He was followed in the 17th Century by a group of painters whose work was much admired while they lived—José de Ribera, Francisco de Zurbarán, and Bartolomé Estéban Murillo. Ribera was a violent man who pictured penitents, saints, beggars and Madonnas with a disturbing realism. Zurbarán was a painter of austerely composed monastic and religious life. Murillo was visionary but sentimental. In the 18th Century, he was widely regarded as one of the greatest of Spanish painters.

Many critics today, however, would say that Spain's most distinguished painter is Diego Rodríguez de Silva y Velázquez (1599-1660). Cool, aristocratic and objective, he was a realist who allowed no sentimentality to reach his clear, logical canvases. These characteristics give his work a warmth and dignity that is supremely Spanish. In his *Maids of Honor*, for example, he paints a court dwarf with neither flattery nor pity, something few other painters could bring off. He was court painter to Philip IV, and he left behind him more than a hundred canvases that had considerable influence on the 19th Century impressionists.

Creating an academy dedicated to the advancement of fine arts often results in discouraging creative imagination and paralyzing effort. In 1752 Ferdinand VI did just that. No sooner had the San Fernando Royal Academy of Fine Arts been founded than painting of any real significance practically disappeared in Spain until modern times.

In the middle of this academic atmosphere stood one gigantic figure. His name was Francisco José de Goya y Lucientes. A proud individualist with the instinct of a major novelist, he had a frank and spontaneous personality. The son of humble parents, Goya was a strong, bull-necked, tousle-headed young man with a strong jaw and deep brown eyes. He was restless, he was volcanic, he worked in epic spurts, sometimes, it is said, by candlelight.

D URING the latter half of his life he was stone deaf. Legend has it that many of the women he painted he knew in the Biblical sense, undoubtedly convincing them one by one that an artist cannot do a vibrant portrait of a woman without experiencing her fully. He is believed to have sired 20 children.

One portrait he executed with particular brilliance was of the 35-year-old Duchess of Alba.

On her right hand there are two engraved rings —one says "Alba," the other says "Goya." She is pointing toward the ground where, sketched in the earth, is Goya's name.

Goya said that his three masters were "Velázquez, Rembrandt and Nature." His work ran a wide gamut: it was narrative and decorative, realistic and religious, theatrical and satirical. As a body, it is perhaps the best social commentary extant on the world he lived in—a world that was almost as changing as the 20th Century. Goya's oils and sketches began during the quiet lull before the French Revolution and continued through years of violence that included Napoleon's invasion of Spain. His celebrated portrait of Wellington was done in 1812 while the Iron Duke was busy waging his successful peninsular campaign. The greatest interpreter of his own age, Goya has been called "the father of the modern spirit in art."

ARCHITECTURE, like painting and literature, had its periods of transition. When Philip II came to the throne in 1556, plateresque, a highly ornamental architectural style, was in popular favor. But Philip II was a serious man who favored a more sober, monumental style. By royal order, buildings of majestic simplicity became the ideal of the period.

The new movement would be exemplified for all time in Philip's royal palace called the Escorial. Huge and imposing, it stands on a plain some 30 miles northwest of Madrid. It is part church, part monastery and part mausoleum, with apartments and offices of state. Its somber austerity expresses the Spanish preoccupation with the idea of death.

Inevitably, there had to be a reaction to this austerity in architecture. It came in the 17th Century with Spanish baroque, which culminated in the so-called Churrigueresque (named for architect José Churriguera). The buildings of this period are full of rich color, exuberant designs, twisted columns, inverted obelisks, gold-encrusted altars and luxuriant façades.

Soon after the Bourbons took over the Spanish throne in 1700, influences from France and Italy began to creep into Spanish architecture. Philip V was born French, the grandson of Louis XIV. His second wife was an Italian, and she dominated his court with her Italian tastes. Perhaps the best example of the architecture that resulted is La Granja, the royal hunting lodge near Madrid. Originally Spanish, it was remodeled after Italian designs and the landscaping is copied from the gardens at Versailles.

After Philip's time, nothing of architectural significance happened in Spain until the general European artistic renaissance of the late 19th and early 20th Centuries. Then, in Catalonia, there emerged an exotic genius whose work is unique in his or any other time. Antonio Gaudí's Church of the Holy Family in Barcelona, begun in 1882, has never been finished. But even unfinished, it is a spectacular example of engineering. Its towering east wall, topped by four rocket-like spires, is an original triumph that mingles neo-Gothic and turn-of-the-century *art nouveau*.

Spanish artists of the modern era, while no less startling than Gaudí, are far better known outside Spain. Notable in this group are the Catalan modern, Joan Miró, with his language of whimsical and colorful hieroglyphics; the late cubist Juan Gris; and Salvador Dali, a surrealist who is a superb draftsman and also has a real talent for self-publicity.

THE most prodigious artistic talent of the 20th Century is Pablo Picasso. Born in Málaga, he settled permanently in Paris when he was 23. His work is permeated with Spanish feeling, but in a sense, Picasso is not really a Spaniard: he is an International. So too is Cristóbal Balenciaga, whose Paris salon has long stood at the very pinnacle of *haute couture*.

Musically, Spain is a country that is rich in tradition and relatively poor in composers. Tomás Luis de Victoria (c.1548-1611) was one of Palestrina's great contemporaries. The pianist-composer Isaac Albéniz (1860-1909) wrote brilliant pianoforte pieces such as the suite *Iberia*, which reproduces traditional rhythms of popular Spanish music. The late Manuel de Falla merits recognition among the great modern composers of Europe. His lifelong goal was "to glorify the immortality of Spain through music." He did so with such uniquely Iberian compositions as his ballets *El Amor Brujo* (Love, the Sorcerer) and *Three-Cornered Hat* and his cantata *Atlántida*.

SPANISH instrumentalists have often been the best in their fields, like the cellist Pablo Casals and the guitarist Andrés Segovia today. But the deepest traditions of Spanish music are known only slightly to the outside world. Spaniards are enormously fond of their zarzuelas, a type of comic operetta that first developed in the 17th Century. Various troupes have carried flamenco music and dance outside of Spain, but at its best this art form needs the atmosphere of the gypsy caves it comes from. And unique to the Spanish south is the *cante hondo*, the deep song that bypasses the lesser passions and appeals directly to the soul.

In the 19th Century, Spain followed other European countries along the paths of Romanticism, particularly in the theater and in lyric poetry. The great names were Espronceda, Zorrilla and Bécquer. Toward the middle of the last century, realism became the reigning fashion in fiction, and in Benito Pérez Galdós Spain produced an outstanding novelist.

The cultural renaissance that began early in the 20th Century produced some of the most serious thinkers in Spanish literature, men like poet-essayist Miguel de Unamuno and philosopher José Ortega y Gasset, who were vitally concerned with the social and political course of their nation. Ortega y Gasset felt that no nation could succeed unless it was directed by "a select minority." The select man, he said, was one "who makes great demands on himself." He described Spain as sinking into a "long coma of egotism and idiocy. . . . Today we are not so much a people as a cloud of dust that was left in the air when a great people went galloping down the highroad of history."

The cultural renaissance also produced the lyric poet Antonio Machado, the poet Juan Ramón Jiménez, who won the Nobel Prize for literature in 1956, and Pío Baroja, considered by many to be one of Spain's most important contemporary novelists. But by far the greatest name of Spanish culture in the 20th Century is Federico García Lorca, the tragic poet of Andalusia who was shot by Franco supporters at the outbreak of the Civil War. Born in 1898 in a village near Granada, García Lorca was the son of a prosperous landowner and a schoolteacher. The legends and songs of Andalusia entered his blood in his boyhood and reemerged in some of the most stirring lyric poetry ever written. His talent was so refined that he could draw considerable emotion out of the sparest line or fragment of dialogue. In addition to poetry, García Lorca wrote plays, notably *Yerma, Blood Wedding* and *The House of Bernarda Alba*—all deeply brooding, concerned with basic matters of life and death, and bathed in blood and symbolism.

BOTH in the theater and in individual poems, García Lorca was considered by Spaniards the most moving lyric poet since Spain's literary golden age. His images were something more than arresting: "When all the rooftops are nothing but furrows on the earth, dawn shrugs her shoulders in a vast profile of stone." His dark vision was expressed in primary colors—nature, sex, death, life.

His strong voice, sad and quiet, was the voice of Spain. Other writers had found it before him, but it had not been heard so clearly for 300 years:

> *Upon the bare mountain*
> *   a calvary.*
> *Clear water*
> *   and centennial olive trees.*
> *Through the narrow streets*
> *   cloaked men go,*
> *   and in the towers*
> *   vanes are rotating.*
> *Eternally rotating.*
> *O lost village*
> *In the Andalusia of weeping!*

NOVELIST Camilo José Cela portrays the desperations of Spain's poor with such unrelenting realism that his works have been suppressed at times by the government.

NOVELIST José María Gironella is best known for his 1953 book *The Cypresses Believe in God*, a detailed and moving account of life in Spain just before the Civil War.

A Penetrating, Vibrant Culture

Spain has not had so many brilliant artists as France or Italy, or so many profound writers as England. But when great Spanish artists and writers have appeared, their work has had an intense power that has made it the equal of any. In few other countries have creative individuals experimented so boldly to extend the capacities of their art or so consistently attempted to see beyond the appearance of things and penetrate to a deeper reality—to answer, or at least ask, the ultimate human and spiritual questions. It is typical of Spain that its most renowned writer, Cervantes, wrote of a madman in whom the real world and a world of fantasy intertwine.

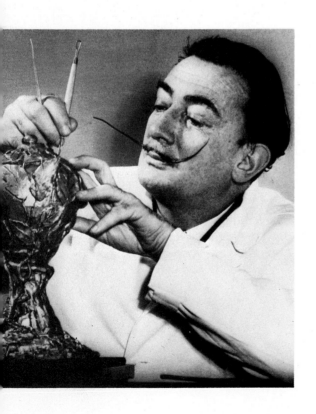

MUSICIAN Andrés Segovia, who is one of the greatest of concert stars, helped make the six-string Spanish guitar the most popular instrument in the Western world.

ARTIST Salvador Dali, world famed for his surrealist paintings, also models jeweled figures in a New York studio. Dali returns frequently to his native Catalonia.

YOUNG DESIGNER Elio Berhanyer, once a farm laborer, *(opposite)* is one of several talented couturiers who have made Madrid a center of interest in the world of fashion.

YOUNG PAINTER Antonio Tàpies of Barcelona brought international recognition to avant-garde Spanish art by winning two top prizes at the Venice Biennale in 1958.

135

PAINTING *became a Spanish national glory in the 16th and 17th Centuries,* *starting with the work of El Greco and the establishment of a royal collection*

GREAT ART MUSEUM, the Prado in Madrid impresses a priest who stands before El Greco's *The Pentecost*. Many of the Prado's paintings were amassed by Spanish kings.

BRILLIANT CANVAS by El Greco shows the Count Orgaz being entombed by St. Stephen *(left)* and St. Augustine. The artist himself is shown above St. Stephen's head.

MURILLO prospered as a favorite painter among the wealthy and pious Seville society of the 17th Century. His rather saccharine style is evident in a canvas *(right)* of a youthful St. Thomas of Villanueva giving his clothes to beggar boys.

ZURBARAN, like Murillo, devoted his efforts to religious painting. The austerity of his art can be seen in his *Flight into Egypt (below)*, which depicts the Holy Family as ordinary Spanish peasants saying good-bye to village neighbors.

VELAZQUEZ spent 37 years as court painter to Philip IV. In 1656 he executed an enormous portrait *(opposite)* of Princess Margarita, her ladies in waiting, dwarfs and pet dog. Using two mirrors he included himself and the king and queen *(in rear)*.

THE DUCHESS OF ALBA appears in a great Francisco de Goya portrait *(opposite)* painted in 1797. They may have been lovers: Goya linked their names on her rings.

THE DUKE OF WELLINGTON was painted by Goya after his victory at Salamanca. The portrait was stolen from Britain's National Gallery in 1961 and later returned.

A CUBIST STILL LIFE of his room and window in Paris
was painted by Juan Gris in 1915. Like Joan Miró *(page
124)* and Pablo Picasso, Gris left Spain when he was
young to study painting in Paris and became identified
with the early French moderns. Before his death in 1927,
Gris was recognized as a pioneer in the cubist movement.

A DANCING FAUN tries hard to amuse a sober sea nymph
as Pan pipes the tune in this 1938 oil by Pablo Picasso.
Most of the work Picasso did during the Civil War was
more tormented than this canvas which, however, seems
to mock man's attempts to achieve love and happiness.
The painting is part of Picasso's own personal collection.

A MODERN RENAISSANCE *was spurred by the provocative work*

of a number of daring and original Spanish-born painters

10

On the Threshold of Europe

THE story of Spain in recent years is one of considerable economic advance, accompanied by major changes in living habits. A people traditionally given to asceticism have shown themselves eager to acquire the material benefits that other Western peoples enjoy. It appears that the Spaniard in the old days didn't sit in his doorway strumming his guitar because he particularly wanted to; before now there just wasn't much else to do. Today millions are experiencing the excitements of television and automobiles and city apartments—and sometimes even paid vacations.

Prosperity came after 1959, with the relaxa-

tion of government controls on business and the opening of Spain's frontiers to the passage of goods and people and money. It came so fast that the Franco government hardly knew what was happening. James Morris has described the irony of the situation in the London magazine *Encounter:* "General Franco's regime . . . came to power as the champion of traditional Spanishness, dedicated to the proposition that materialism, like cosmopolitanism, liberalism, or communism, was necessarily damaging to Spanish ideals. God, Spain, Chivalry, Death were the high-sounding watchwords of the Caudillo's cause. Patriotism of the old kind,

145

Christianity of the Spanish sort—these were its driving forces. The Crusade was intended to keep Spain Spanish, to save her from alien values; but thirty years after its victorious conclusion, its exiled enemies are winning after all. It was the academic liberals who wanted to open the doors of Spain, padlock the Cid's tomb once and for all, and rejoin the world outside; but today the Spanish people at large, who rejected in their time both the Reformation and the French Revolution, are at last beginning to accept what we in the democratic West like to call, with a wry smile or a politician's slogan, *progress*."

CAN progress be limited just to income and consumption, and not extend to the realm of ideas? Can liberalization of the Spanish economy continue and expand without liberalization of the autocratic State?

Ever since the United States offered Franco a hand of friendship in 1953 to begin the chain of events that brought Spain out of its postwar isolation, the regime has been under pressures of many kinds to establish a freer society. Not the least of these pressures has come in the form of tactful suggestions from American diplomats and aid officials. After long years of ostracism, Franco has shown himself extremely anxious to stay on good terms with the United States and to achieve respectability in the eyes of the West as a whole. Many of the modest governmental reforms he made in the mid-1960s can be seen as public relations measures designed to improve the Spanish image abroad.

But there was need also to counter a rising ferment of dissatisfaction within the country. The Europeanization of Spain that proceeded so rapidly after 1959 brought new standards of judgment to many Spaniards—and often a sense of having been cheated. From the millions of tourists who streamed across their borders, the Spanish began to learn that people of other countries enjoy better pay for their work, greater freedom in their daily lives and a stronger voice in their own governments. The hundreds of thousands of Spanish workers who took jobs in other parts of Europe saw this for themselves, and many of them came home to tell about it. Spanish businessmen of the new middle class had enough dealings with the outside world to figure out how and why Spain, in comparison with other countries, was still a backward nation.

One of the important areas in which the Franco regime moved to head off criticism was labor relations. Historians recall that General Franco settled the first strike with which he was ever confronted—an uprising in the coal region of Asturias in 1934—by the simple expedient of ordering 2,000 miners shot. For decades strikes of any kind in Spain were considered subversive, to be put down brutally when they occurred. But in 1965 the regime proclaimed that thenceforth workers had the legal right to strike in support of wage demands. The reason for the about-face was not difficult to find: Spain, seeking entrance to the Common Market, had no chance of succeeding as long as its repressive labor policies gave offense to the international trade union organizations which strongly influence Western European parliaments. Trade unionists are still hostile toward the Spanish *sindicatos* that function as one giant company union for the whole country. For this reason the regime began to study the possibility of overhauling the entire *sindicato* setup, a development that could bring some change in the existing labor-management-government relationship.

THEN there was the matter of censorship, which set Spain conspicuously apart from the democratic nations. Foreign residents in Madrid and other cities have long been scornful of the censored Spanish press, in which trivial ceremonies involving local bishops and generals pass for news: "Byzantine newspaper reports on all possible inaugurations and jubilees," as one visiting Swiss journalist described it. For decades, to print anything without the approval of the Franco regime was an invitation to a jail sentence. But in 1966 Franco's rubber-stamp legislature, the *cortes,* passed a law putting a stop to the prepublication censorship of newspapers (but not affecting censorship of the more influential radio, television and movies). The much-advertised press law does little to end subservience of the Spanish press to the regime, which exercises control through subsidizing newsprint costs and licensing editors. The law calls for obedience to "the principles of the National Movement," and editors can be suspended or fined for infractions. It will be a long time before anything like a free press exists in Spain. But a small step was taken in the direction of freedom.

THROUGH actions of this sort, Franco appeared to be attempting to appease his critics with minor concessions here and there, yielding slightly to the most compelling pressures, without changing the essential character of the regime. Most observers prophesied that things would go along in much the same manner as long as Franco remained in power—with the old man handing out carefully measured doses of liberty from time to time in palliation of minor political aches and pains, while the Army, the Falange and the Church maintained the status quo. General Franco once spoke of himself as the Abraham Lincoln of Spain, who had given the country its "final shape."

The opposition to Franco, once hopefully predicted by exiled Republican leaders, has never developed as an effective force in Spanish life, and the exiles themselves now seem no more than faint voices out of a remote past. In the cities of Spain, historically nurturing grounds for political agitation, the radicalism of factory workers has been damped by prosperity. In the depressed countryside, farmers are unorganized, inarticulate and in the habit of taking their opinions from the landowners and the clergy. The students and other intellectuals have clamored now and again about civil liberties, but then, when have students ever been satisfied with their lot? The only potentially serious crack in the solidarity of Franco's support has come from a division within the Spanish Church, swept in recent years by tides of

ecumenicism and social consciousness emanating from Rome. The Spanish hierarchy—cardinals and bishops whose average age is 68—still firmly align themselves with the regime, but some of the younger clergy have emerged as strongly outspoken critics.

"Priests Clubbed by Spanish Police," declared newspaper headlines in many languages around the world in May 1966. Students at the University of Barcelona, marching to protest the beating of one of their leaders in prison, were joined by more than 100 priests—and Franco's security forces broke up the whole demonstration with considerable brutality. The incident contained so many of the basic elements of contemporary Spanish life that it could be seen almost as the story of Spain in microcosm. There were the intellectuals striving for freedom from regimentation, the club-swinging cops, the idealistic young clergymen devoted to human rights, a septuagenarian bishop responsive to a different voice of conscience, and within the whole drama an echo of the age-old separatist tendency of Catalonia, centered in Barcelona, capital of that ancient province.

THE "principles of the National Movement" have required that students, professors and administrators at any Spanish university be herded together into one branch of a nationwide educational *sindicato* under the direction of the Falange, which could be relied upon to guard the student mind from subversion and hound out of university life any faculty member tainted with "progressive" ideas. All over Spain, politically-minded groups of students have repeatedly rioted for the right to choose their own representatives in these union-type organizations or to establish their own organizations instead. The Barcelona incident in the Spring of 1966 was but one of many student-police clashes.

In this instance Franco reacted swiftly by closing down the 17,000-member university (the second largest in Spain). But 120 priests had been manhandled, a violation of canon law, and the bruised clergymen petitioned 76-year-old Archbishop Gregorio Modrego y Casaus to properly punish the offending policemen by excommunication. The archbishop, no doubt, had heard from Madrid; he temporized, urged everyone to keep calm, and ended by doing nothing. All over the nation the Spanish press, although newly released from official censorship, spoke with familiar unanimity: a group of Barcelona priests, readers were told, had been guilty of "tumultuous" actions in a public place, which added up to "most unpriestly conduct." There was a suggestion that the whole thing had to do with illegal Catalonian agitation for secession, no explanation of the real reason for the student demonstration in the first place, and not a hint that the priests had been clubbed and kicked by Franco's police.

THERE may be other difficulties for the Franco regime in holding back the advance of human freedoms, as Spain moves further out into the mainstream of European thought and opinion. But no serious student of Spanish affairs expects Franco to be displaced as chief of state in his lifetime. A vast number of middle-aged and elderly Spaniards admire him as the man who has maintained order for a quarter of a century. He has preserved a more stable Spain, for a longer period, than has existed for several centuries. For the majority of Spaniards—those not tied to the land—the most recent years of Franco's rule have brought increasing fortune, and the Caudillo naturally gets the credit for this. Nothing suggests that his skill at political maneuver is declining. As yet he has not overreached. Franco has never been an expansionist or an imperialist (like other Fascist dictators), and he never shared enthusiastically in the various extreme Falangist ambitions to create a new Hispanic world empire. The internal policy of his regime has aimed at controlling the working of the system—nominally at least—in the public interest.

To an extraordinary degree, Franco is immune from criticism as an individual. Spaniards who have complaints against their government —and there are many—tend to find fault with some minister or bureau within the regime, or to blame the regime itself impersonally; the Caudillo stands somehow above the hurly-burly of daily events.

After Franco, what?

There will almost certainly be a king. It could be Don Juan, the Pretender. But Franco has shown increasing favor to the Pretender's son, Prince Juan Carlos, who might be persuaded to ascend the throne after reaching the required age of 30 in 1968. To administer the future government, there is talk of setting up a premier of sorts, who might assume some of the functions exercised by the Caudillo during his lifetime. But there is wrangling within the regime over the question of how such a premier should be chosen. Meanwhile uncertainty about the succession is a cloud that increasingly shadows the national life.

Some observers look optimistically for an early evolution of representative government in Spain after Franco departs. They visualize a broadly based Christian Democratic party, on the model of that found in Italy, holding power in a new Republic—perhaps with Ruiz Jiménez as prime minister. Others recall the old political contrariness of the Spaniard and think of all the irreconcilable conflicts that exist among Carlists, Monarchists, Falangists, Christian Democrats of numerous diverse tendencies, Socialists of equal heterogeneity, National Syndicalists and Communists. They find reason to believe that Franco's passing will usher in a period of severe conflict in Spanish public life.

BUT memories of the Civil War are too vivid to allow for another total breakdown —and Spain today has too much at stake in its new prosperity. Faced with any likelihood of political violence, the army can be expected to step in with a *pronunciamento* to maintain order—and the end result could well be the establishment of a new dictatorship.

"What Spain needs," writes the editor of a Falangist newspaper, "is another Franco."

Tourists on the Costa Brava pass above peasant women mending fish nets. Next page: A modern apartment house rises in Madrid.

THE WORLD MOVES IN *on the consciousness of a Spain long quiescent . . .*

. . . and now reaching for the physical treasures of the 20th Century—material

benefits with which may come profound changes in the social and political order

Appendix

HISTORICAL DATES

<table>
<tr><td>B.C.</td><td></td></tr>
<tr><td>Paleolithic age</td><td>In the Altamira cave paintings near Santander, Cro-Magnon man depicts his hunt for food</td></tr>
<tr><td>11th Century</td><td>Phoenicians establish a trading post at Gadir (Cadiz)</td></tr>
<tr><td>7th-6th Centuries</td><td>Celtic tribes cross the Pyrenees into Spain</td></tr>
<tr><td>6th Century</td><td>Greeks form colonies and dispute choice regions with the Phoenicians. Carthaginians, coming from Africa to aid their sister colony, stay on as conquerors</td></tr>
<tr><td>218-201</td><td>Rome destroys Carthage's power in the Second Punic War, and the peninsula is later divided into Roman provinces</td></tr>
<tr><td>A.D.</td><td></td></tr>
<tr><td>2nd-3rd Centuries</td><td>Christian communities develop in Spain</td></tr>
<tr><td>409</td><td>Vandal, Suevi and Alan tribesmen invade from the north, sweeping away Roman social order</td></tr>
<tr><td>414</td><td>Visigoths follow the other Germanic tribes, ultimately conquering or forcing them out</td></tr>
<tr><td>589</td><td>Roman Catholicism is proclaimed the Visigothic state religion after the conversion of King Reccared from Arian Christianity</td></tr>
<tr><td>711-718</td><td>Encouraged by enemies of King Roderick, Moslems from North Africa attack and defeat the Visigoths, swiftly conquer all but small northern mountain regions of the peninsula</td></tr>
<tr><td>c.718</td><td>The Reconquista begins when Pelayo, a Visigoth nobleman, leads a few straggling Christian armies to victory over Moslem forces in the Asturian mountains. His successors struggle for 800 years to regain the other Moslem holdings</td></tr>
<tr><td>756</td><td>Abdul Rahman, an Arab prince fleeing the overthrow of his family in Syria, conquers Cordova and establishes a dynasty</td></tr>
<tr><td>801</td><td>Charlemagne and his son, Louis the Pious, capture Barcelona and organize a Frankish province called the Spanish March</td></tr>
<tr><td>1031</td><td>The Moslem empire disintegrates into feuding petty states. Christians, fired with crusading zeal, make decisive gains</td></tr>
<tr><td>1085</td><td>Toledo is captured from the Moslems by Alfonso VI</td></tr>
<tr><td>1094</td><td>El Cid Campeador, later to become Spain's national hero, takes Valencia, although after his death Moslems regain the city</td></tr>
<tr><td>1143</td><td>Portugal forces recognition of independence from Castile</td></tr>
<tr><td>1230-1246</td><td>Castile and León united. The ruler of the new kingdom, Ferdinand III, conquers Cordova and Seville</td></tr>
<tr><td>1309</td><td>Union of Aragon and Valencia</td></tr>
<tr><td>1479</td><td>Aragon and Castile are united under the joint rule of Ferdinand and Isabella, the "Catholic Sovereigns"</td></tr>
<tr><td>1480</td><td>The Inquisition is introduced</td></tr>
<tr><td>1492</td><td>Granada, the Moslems' last Spanish holding, falls to the Christians. Columbus plants the banner of the Catholic Sovereigns on New World soil. The Jews are expelled from Spain</td></tr>
<tr><td>1516-1556</td><td>Reign of Charles I, grandson of Ferdinand and Isabella and the first Hapsburg ruler of Spain. He is also crowned Holy Roman Emperor as Charles V. Spain becomes a leading maritime power and embarks upon colonization of the Americas</td></tr>
<tr><td>1556-1598</td><td>During Philip II's reign Spain reaches its zenith of power and influence. Portugal is again annexed, bringing all the peninsula under one rule</td></tr>
<tr><td>1588</td><td>England defeats the Armada, delivering a shattering blow to Spanish prestige</td></tr>
<tr><td>1609-1611</td><td>Half a million Moriscos (Christianized Moslems) are expelled</td></tr>
<tr><td>1621-1700</td><td>Unsuccessful wars waged by Philip IV and Charles II cause further decline of Spanish power. Portugal breaks away</td></tr>
<tr><td>1700-1714</td><td>Charles II bequeaths the empire to Louis XIV's grandson, Philip V, introducing the House of Bourbon to the Spanish throne and leading to the War of the Spanish Succession</td></tr>
<tr><td>1805</td><td>Under French influence Spain is drawn into the conflict between Britain and Napoleon. Britain's Lord Nelson destroys the Franco-Spanish fleet at Trafalgar</td></tr>
<tr><td>1808-1812</td><td>Napoleon places his brother Joseph on the Spanish throne, touching off guerrilla action against the French occupation forces. The cortes (parliament)</td></tr>
<tr><td></td><td>meets in Cadiz and drafts the first national constitution</td></tr>
<tr><td>1813</td><td>Napoleon, after the Duke of Wellington's victory at Vitoria, recalls his troops, recognizes Ferdinand VII as king</td></tr>
<tr><td>1814-1833</td><td>Ferdinand abrogates the constitution, tries to destroy the liberals. South American colonies bid for independence</td></tr>
<tr><td>1833-1840</td><td>Disputes over the succession between Ferdinand's daughter, Infanta Isabella, and his brother, Don Carlos, cause the first Carlist War. Don Carlos is defeated and leaves Spain</td></tr>
<tr><td>1868</td><td>Rebellion against Isabella's irresponsible rule forces her into exile</td></tr>
<tr><td>1874</td><td>After further conflicts with Carlists and a brief experiment as a republic, the country enthrones Isabella's son, Alfonso XII</td></tr>
<tr><td>1898</td><td>Spain loses Puerto Rico, the Philippines and Cuba in the Spanish-American War</td></tr>
<tr><td>1912</td><td>Spanish protectorate is recognized in Morocco</td></tr>
<tr><td>1923</td><td>The Captain General of Catalonia, Primo de Rivera, takes over as dictator of Spain unopposed by King Alfonso XIII</td></tr>
<tr><td>1927</td><td>Riff revolts in Morocco, led by Abdul Krim, are crushed by a French-Spanish operation</td></tr>
<tr><td>1931</td><td>The Second Republic is proclaimed after municipal elections are held. Alfonso XIII leaves Spain</td></tr>
<tr><td>1933</td><td>Falange party founded</td></tr>
<tr><td>1936</td><td>The Popular Front, an alliance of the Left, wins general elections</td></tr>
<tr><td>1936-1939</td><td>Strikes, riots and armed revolts by bitterly opposing political factions flame into Civil War. General Francisco Franco, heading a rightist Insurgent government in Burgos, eventually triumphs, aided by Hitler and Mussolini</td></tr>
<tr><td>1947</td><td>The Law of Succession, making Spain a monarchy, is approved in a national referendum. It provides for a member of the royal family to succeed Franco</td></tr>
<tr><td>1953</td><td>Pact for the establishment of U.S. bases in Spain is signed</td></tr>
<tr><td>1955</td><td>Spain is admitted to the U.N.</td></tr>
<tr><td>1956</td><td>The Spanish protectorate in Morocco is abolished</td></tr>
<tr><td>1964</td><td>Spain's first four-year plan of economic development (1964-1967) is inaugurated</td></tr>
</table>

FOR FURTHER READING

CHAPTER 1: THE SPANISH PERSONALITY

Altamira, Rafael, *A History of Spain*. D. Van Nostrand, 1949.

Aubier, Dominique, and Manuel Tuñon de Lara, *Spain*. Viking Press, 1960.

Bertrand, Louis, and Sir Charles Petrie, *The History of Spain*. Macmillan, 1952.

Borrow, George, *The Bible in Spain*. Dufour Editions, 1959.

Brenan, Gerald, *The Face of Spain*. Cambridge University Press, 1960.

Chapman, Charles E., *A History of Spain*. Macmillan, 1961.

Crockett, Lucy H., *Kings Without Castles*. Rand McNally, 1957.

Livermore, Harold, *History of Spain*. Farrar, Straus and Cudahy, 1958.

Peers, Edgar Allison, ed., *Spain: A Companion to Spanish Studies*. Pitman Publishing, 1957.

Sitwell, Sacheverell, *Spain*. Hastings House Publishers, 1955.

Trend, John B., *The Civilization of Spain*. Oxford University Press, 1944.

CHAPTER 2: HISTORY TO 1492

Castro, Americo, *The Structure of Spanish History*. Princeton University Press, 1954.

Dixon, Pierson, *Iberians of Spain and Their Relations with the Aegean World*. Oxford University Press, 1940.

Hole, Edwyn, *Andalus, Spain Under the Muslims*. Dufour Editions, 1958.

Irving, Washington, *The Conquest of Granada*. Everyman's Library, 1941.

Trend, John B., *The Origins of Modern Spain*. Macmillan, 1934.

Wiseman, Francis J., *Roman Spain*. Macmillan, 1956.

Wright, Richard, *Pagan Spain*. Harper & Brothers, 1957.

CHAPTER 3: AN ERA OF GREATNESS

Davies, R. Trevor, *The Golden Century of Spain, 1501-1621*. St. Martin's Press, 1954.

Haring, Clarence Henry, *The Spanish Empire in America*. Oxford University Press, 1947.

Hume, M.A.S., *Spain, 1479-1788*. Cambridge University Press, 1913.

Kany, Charles E., *Life and Manners in Madrid, 1750-1800*. University of California Press, 1932.

Madariaga, Salvador de, *The Rise of the Spanish American Empire*. Macmillan, 1947. *The Fall of the Spanish American Empire*. Macmillan, 1948.

Mariéjol, Jean H., *The Spain of Ferdinand and Isabella*. Rutgers University Press, 1961.

Merriman, Roger B., *The Rise of the Spanish Empire in the Old World and in the New*. Macmillan, 1936.

CHAPTER 4: DECLINE AND DISASTER

Brenan, Gerald, *The Spanish Labyrinth*. Cambridge University Press, 1950.

Jackson, Gabriel, *The Spanish Republic and the Civil War*. Princeton University Press, 1965.

Matthews, Herbert L., *The Yoke and the Arrows*. Braziller, 1961.

Orwell, George, *Homage to Catalonia*. Beacon Press, 1955.

Paul, Elliot, *The Life and Death of a Spanish Town*. Modern Library, 1942.

Peers, Edgar Allison, *The Spanish Tragedy, 1930-36*. Oxford University Press, 1936.

Puzzo, Dante A., *Spain and the Great Powers*. Columbia University Press, 1962.

Ramos Oliveira, Antonio, *Politics, Economics and Men of Modern Spain, 1808-1946*. Crown Publishers, 1948.

Taylor, Foster Jay, *The United States and the Spanish Civil War*. Bookman Associates, 1956.

Thomas, Hugh, *The Spanish Civil War*. Harper & Brothers, 1961.

CHAPTERS 5 AND 7: POLITICS

Alba, Victor, *Sleepless Spain*. Cobbett Press, London, 1948.

Arrarás, Joaquín, *Francisco Franco: The Times and the Man*. Bruce Publishing, 1938.

Feis, Herbert, *The Spanish Story: Franco and the Nations at War*. Alfred A. Knopf, 1948.

Fischer, Louis, *Men and Politics*. Duell, Sloan & Pearce, 1941.

Hamilton, Thomas Jefferson, *Appeasement's Child: The Franco Regime in Spain*. Alfred A. Knopf, 1943.

Hughes, Emmet John, *Report from Spain*. Henry Holt, 1947.

Madariaga, Salvador de, *Spain, A Modern History*. Frederick A. Praeger, 1958.

Payne, Stanley, *Falange: A History of Spanish Fascism*. Stanford University Press, 1961.

CHAPTER 6: THE ECONOMY

Carr, Richard Comyns, "Spain's Economic Situation." *The World Today*, Vol. 18, No. 5 (May 1962).

Girbau-Léon, Vicente, "The Economic Background of the Spanish Situation." *The World Today*, Vol. 16, No. 9 (September 1960).

Organization for Economic Cooperation and Development Surveys, *Spain*, 1962.

Whitaker, Arthur P., *Spain and Defense of the West*. Harper & Brothers, 1961.

CHAPTER 8: TOWN AND VILLAGE LIFE

Barea, Arturo, *The Forging of a Rebel*. Reynal, 1946.

Brenan, Gerald, *South from Granada*. Farrar, Straus & Cudahy, 1957.

Cleugh, James, *Image of Spain*. George G. Harrap, 1961.

Pitt-Rivers, J. A., *The People of the Sierra*. Criterion Books, 1954.

Pritchett, Victor Sawdon, *The Spanish Temper*. Alfred A. Knopf, 1954.

CHAPTER 9: CULTURE AND THE ARTS

Brenan, Gerald, *The Literature of the Spanish People*. Cambridge University Press, 1953.

Chandler, Richard E., and Kessel Schwartz, *A New History of Spanish Literature*. Louisiana State University Press, 1961.

Chase, Gilbert, *The Music of Spain*. Dover Publications, 1959.

Collins, George R., *Antonio Gaudí*. George Braziller, 1960.

Hughes, Russell M., *Spanish Dancing*. A. S. Barnes, 1948.

King, G., *Heart of Spain*. Harvard University Press, 1941.

Kubler, George, and Martin Soria, *Art and Architecture in Spain and Portugal and their American Dominions 1500-1800*. Penguin Books, 1959.

Lassaigne, Jacques, *Spanish Painting: From the Catalan Frescos to El Greco*. Skira, 1952. *Spanish Painting: From Velazquez to Picasso*. Skira, 1952.

Martinez-Lopez, Ramon, ed., *Image of Spain: a special edition of The Texas Quarterly*. University of Texas, 1961.

Northup, George T., *An Introduction to Spanish Literature*. University of Chicago Press, 1960.

O'Hara, Frank, *New Spanish Painting and Sculpture*. The Museum of Modern Art, 1960.

Peers, Edgar Allison, ed., *A Critical Anthology of Spanish Verse*. University of California Press, 1949.

Turnbull, Eleanor L., ed., *Ten Centuries of Spanish Poetry*. Johns Hopkins Press, 1955.

CHAPTER 10: EVOLVING SPAIN

Cleugh, James, *Spain in the Modern World*. Alfred A. Knopf, 1953.

Hayes, Carlton J. H., *The United States and Spain: An Interpretation*. Sheed & Ward, 1951.

Welles, Benjamin, *Spain, The Gentle Anarchy*. Frederick A. Praeger, 1965.

Whitaker, Arthur P., *Spain and Defense of the West*. Harper & Brothers, 1961.

FAMOUS SPANISH CULTURAL FIGURES AND THEIR PRINCIPAL WORKS

MUSIC

Encina, Juan del	1468-1529	Songs for his pastoral plays
Narvaéz, Luis de	16th Century	Compositions for the lutelike vihuela
Morales, Cristóbal	c.1500-1553	Penitential motet: *Emendemus in melius.* Masses, cantatas, madrigals
Milán, Luis	c.1500-c.1561	Ballads for voice and lute
Victoria, Tomás Luis de	c. 1548-1611	Masses, motets, magnificats, hymns in contrapuntal style
Martín y Soler, Vicente	1754-1806	Operas: *Una Cosa Rara, Ifigenia in Aulide.* Ballets, church music
Sor, Fernando	1778-1839	Guitarist and composer. Fantasies, minuets and studies for guitar
Pedrell, Felipe	1841-1922	Operas: *Los Pirineos, La Celestina*
Bretón, Tomás	1850-1923	Zarzuela: *La Verbena de la Paloma.* Operas: *Los Amantes de Teruel, La Dolores*
Albéniz, Isaac	1860-1909	Pianist and composer. Collection of 12 piano pieces: *Iberia.* Opera: *Pepita Jiménez*
Granados, Enrique	1867-1916	Piano suite forming the basis of a later opera: *Goyescas.* Other operas, orchestral works
Falla, Manuel de	1876-1946	Opera: *La Vida Breve.* Ballets: *El Amor Brujo, The Three-Cornered Hat.* Composition for piano and orchestra: *Nights in the Gardens of Spain.* Stage piece for puppets and singers: *El Retablo de Maese Pedro.* Cantata: *La Atlántida*
Casals, Pablo	1876-	Cellist, conductor and composer of symphonic and chamber music
Turina, Joaquín	1882-1949	Orchestral works: *La Procesión del Rocio, Danzas Fantásticas.* Pianoforte pieces
Manén, Joan	1883-	Violinist and composer. Symphonic poems: *Nova Catalonia.* Operas
Esplá, Oscar	1886-	Ballets: *El Contrabandista.* Orchestral works: *Suite Levantina.* Chamber music, piano pieces
Segovia, Andrés	1893-	Classical guitarist. Transcribes early contrapuntal music
Halffter, Rodolfo	1900-	Ballets: *Don Lindo de Almería Obertura Concertante* for piano and orchestra
Halffter, Ernesto	1905-	Conductor and composer. Orchestral works: *Sinfonietta, Portuguese Rhapsody.* Operas, chamber music

PAINTING

Bassa, Ferrer	c.1285-1348	Considered the founder of the Catalan school of painting. Cycle of murals in the Convent of Pedralbes
Huguet, Jaime	c.1415-1492	Catalan Gothic paintings. Retable of San Abdón and San Sennén
Bermejo, Bartolomé	After 1498-?	*Pietà* in Barcelona Cathedral and the central panel of a retable, *St. Dominic of Silos*
Sánchez Coello, Alonso	c.1531-1590	Portraits in mannerist style of Philip II and the Infantes, Carlos and Isabella
El Greco (Domenikos Theotokopoulos)	1541-1614	Anticipated brushwork of impressionists of later centuries. Visionary and apocalyptical canvases with elongated figures. *Burial of Count Orgaz, View of Toledo, Crucifixion, Resurrection*
Ribalta, Francisco	c.1555-1628	Influenced naturalists of the following century with introduction of tenebrist style: *The Last Supper, Christ Bearing His Cross*
Ribera, José de (or Jusepe)	1591-1652	*Jacob's Dream, The Boy with a Club-Foot, Martyrdom of St. Bartholomew*
Zurbarán, Francisco de	1598-1664	Monastic themes. Noted for his simplicity of design and visionary power of his subjects
Velázquez, Diego Rodríguez de Silva y	1599-1660	Ancestor of moderns. Portraits of royalty and Pope Innocent X, *Surrender of Breda, Maids of Honor, The Spinners*
Murillo, Bartolomé Estéban	1618-1682	Sentimental baroque style. Religious images, particularly of Madonnas and Immaculate Conceptions
Valdés Leal, Juan de	1622-1690	Baroque religious and allegorical paintings: *The Assumption of Elias, Death* and *Vanity*
Coello, Claudio	1642-1693	Large, intricate compositions: *Adoration of the Sacred Form* for the sacristy of the Escorial
Palomino, Antonio	1655-1726	Allegorical fresco decorations for churches. Also wrote biographies of Spanish artists
Goya y Lucientes, Francisco José de	1746-1828	Portraits of the family of Charles IV and the Duchess of Alba. Strongly impressionistic etchings: *Caprichos, Disasters of War, Bull Fights, Disparates*
Picasso, Pablo	1881-	Leading figure in the modern school of painting. Paintings, murals, etchings and sculptures in a variety of forms and techniques: blue period paintings, *Metamorphoses, Guernica*
Solana, José Gutiérrez	1886-1945	Melancholy themes in a style sometimes resembling Goya's "black paintings": *Reunion at the Café Pombo, The Visit of the Bishop*
Gris, Juan (José Victoriano González)	1887-1927	Cubist *Harlequins* and *Pierrots*
Miró, Joan	1893-	Abstracts with bold and decorative effects: *Harlequin Carnival, Dog Barking at the Moon.* Murals, sculpture
Dali, Salvador	1904-	Surrealistic paintings, illustrations: *The Persistence of Memory, The Specter of Sex Appeal.* Religious themes: *The Crucifixion, The Last Supper*
Tàpies, Antonio	1923-	*Three Stains on Grey Space, Graffiti on Blackish Ochre Relief, Space*

SCULPTURE AND ARCHITECTURE

Bartolomé, Maestre	13th Century	Gothic sculpture: apostles on the façade of Tarragona Cathedral
Castayls, Jaime de	14th Century	Gothic sculpture: completed the façade of Tarragona Cathedral
Berruguete, Alonso	c.1488-1561	Mannerist sculpture: forerunner of baroque stylists. Altar screens for San Benito el Real in Valladolid, choir stalls of the Toledo Cathedral and the marble tomb of Cardinal Tavera
Siloë, Diego de	c.1495-1563	Sculpture and architecture: Escalera Dorada in Burgos Cathedral
Gil de Ontañón, Rodrigo	c.1500-1577	Plateresque architecture: Monterrey Palace in Salamanca
Bautista de Toledo, Juan	?-1567	Architecture: designed and commenced work on the Escorial

154

Becerra, Gaspar	c.1520-1570	Sculpture: retable in Astorga Cathedral
Herrera, Juan de	c.1530-1597	Architecture: associated with the *estilo desornamentado* of the Escorial, which he completed. Cathedral of Valladolid
Montañes, Juan Martínez	1568-1649	Sculpture: polychrome Crucifixion and Immaculate Conception statues in wood
Hernández, Gregorio	c.1570-1636	Sculpture: exponent of naturalism and one of the first baroque sculptors
Cano, Alonso	1601-1667	Architecture, sculpture and painting: façade of Granada Cathedral, altar pieces, statuettes and busts
Mena, Pedro de	1628-1693	Sculpture: St. Francis of Assisi in Toledo Cathedral, several Magdalens and Dolorosas
Churriguera, José	1650-1725	Architecture: foremost designer of the late baroque period, also called Churrigueresque after him
Rodríguez, Ventura	1717-1785	Architecture: late baroque style as seen in Pilar Cathedral at Saragossa. Later reverted to austere design
Villanueva, Juan de	1739-1811	Architecture: neoclassical design, most important of which is the Prado in Madrid
Gaudí, Antonio	1852-1926	Architecture: Church of the Sagrada Familia in Barcelona, classified as neo-Catalonian
Torroja, Eduardo	1899-1961	Architecture-engineering: pioneer in the design of concrete shell structure. La Cort Stadium in Barcelona, small churches and shrines
Fisac, Miguel	1913-	Contemporary architecture: Dominican House of Theology at Alcobendas

LITERATURE

Berceo, Gonzalo de	c.1198-c.1265	Poetry: *Life of Santo Domingo de Silos, Miracles of Our Lady*
King Alfonso the Wise	1221-1284	Poetry: *Songs in Praise of the Virgin Mary.* History: *La Crónica General*
Ruiz, Juan	c.1283-c.1350	Poetry: *El Libro de Buen Amor*
Manrique, Jorge	c.1440-1479	Poetry: *Couplets on the Death of His Father*
Vicente, Gil	c.1465-c.1536	Plays: *Amadis, Libila Casandra, Comedia de Rubena*
Garcilaso de la Vega	1503-1536	Poetry: eclogues, elegies, odes and sonnets
Rojas, Fernando de	?-c.1541	Generally considered the author of all but the first of the 16-act tragicomedy, *La Celestina*
Teresa de Jesús, Santa	1515-1582	Autobiography: *Book of My Life.* Mystic philosophy: *The Chambers*
León, Fray Luis de	1527-1591	Poetry: *Serene Night* and *Quiet Life.* Prose: *The Names of Christ*
Cruz, San Juan de la	1542-1591	Mystic poetry and philosophy: *Ascent of Mt. Carmel, Dark Night*
Cervantes Saavedra, Miguel de	1547-1616	Novels: *Don Quixote de La Mancha, Exemplary Novels*
Góngora Argote, Luis de	1561-1627	Poetry: *The Solitudes, The Fables of Polyphemus and Galatea.* Introduced baroque style
Vega Carpio, Félix Lope de	1562-1635	Historical plays: *El Mejor Alcalde el Rey, Fuenteovejuna, The Star of Seville.* Cloak and sword plays: *The Gardener's Dog, Punishment Without Vengeance, The Gentleman from Olmedo*
Castro, Guillén de	1569-1631	Plays: *The Youthful Cid, Deeds of the Cid, Count Alarcos*
Quevedo y Villegas, Francisco de	1580-1645	Picaresque novel: *The Great Knave.* Satirical essay: *The Dreams*
Ruiz de Alarcón, Juan	c.1581-1639	Plays: *The Walls Are Listening, The Suspicious Truth*
Tirso de Molina (Gabriel Téllez)	1584-1648	First to dramatize the Don Juan legend: *The Seducer of Seville.* Other plays: *Prudence of Woman, The Man Damned for Little Faith.* Prose and poetic miscellanies: *The Gardens of Toledo, Pleasant Introduction*
Calderón de la Barca, Pedro	1600-1681	Plays: *Life is a Dream, The Mayor of Zalamea*
Rojas Zorrilla, Francisco de	1607-1648	Play: *None Save the King*
Feijóo, Fray Benito Jerónimo	1676-1764	Essays: *Teatro Crítico Universal, Learned Letters*
Saavedra, Angel de	1791-1865	Narrative poem: *The Foundling Moor.* Romantic drama: *Don Alvaro*
Espronceda, José de	1808-1842	Verse legend: *The Student of Salamanca.* Philosophical poetry: *The Devil World*
Larra, Mariano José de	1809-1837	Satirical essays: *Marry in Haste, Repent at Leisure, Come Back Tomorrow*
Zorrilla, José	1817-1893	Romantic play: *Don Juan Tenorio*
Pereda, José María de	1833-1905	Novels: *Sotileza, Rocks Ahead*
Bécquer, Gustavo Adolfo	1836-1870	Poetry: *Rimas*
Pérez Galdós, Benito	1843-1920	Novels: *Doña Perfecta, Gloria, Fortunata and Jacinta*
Pardo Bazán, Emilia	1852-1921	Novels: *The Ulloa Mansion, Mother Nature, Sunstroke, Melancholy*
Menéndez y Pelayo, Marcelino	1856-1912	Literary history and criticism: *Origins of the Novel, History of Aesthetic Ideas in Spain*
Unamuno, Miguel de	1864-1936	Prose: *The Life of Don Quixote and Sancho, The Tragic Sense of Life.* Poetry: *The Christ of Velásquez*
Benavente, Jacinto	1866-1954	Plays: *The Bonds of Interest, Autumn Roses, The Evildoers of Good*
Blasco Ibáñez, Vicente	1867-1928	Novels: *The Cabin, The Four Horsemen of the Apocalypse, Blood and Sand*
Baroja, Pío	1872-1956	Novels: *Weeds, The Tree of Knowledge*
Azorín	1874-	Memoirs: *Confessions of a Little Philosopher.* Essays: *Spain: Men and Landscapes, Literary Values*
Machado, Antonio	1875-1939	Poetry: *Campos de Castilla, Soledades*
Pérez de Ayala, Ramón	1880-1962	Novels: *Three Poetic Novels, Tigre Juan, Belarmino and Apolonio*
Jiménez, Juan Ramón	1881-1958	Poetry: *Second Poetic Anthology.* Prose: *Platero and I*
Ortega y Gasset, José	1883-1955	Prose: *The Revolt of the Masses.* Criticism: *Meditations on Don Quixote, The Dehumanization of Art*
García Lorca, Federico	1899-1936	Poetry: *Romancero Gitano, Lament for Ignacio Sánchez Mejías, The Poet in New York.* Plays: *Yerma, Blood Wedding, The House of Bernarda Alba*
Sender, Ramón	1902-	Novels: *Before Noon, Mr. Witt Among the Rebels, Seven Red Sundays*
Casona, Alejandro	1903-1965	Plays: *The Beached Mermaid, The Devil Again, Our Natacha*
Cela, Camilo José	1916-	Novels: *The Hive, Pascual Duarte's Family*
Gironella, José María	1917-	Novels: *The Cypresses Believe in God, The Soil Was Shallow*

Credits

The sources for the illustrations in this book are shown below. Credits for pictures from left to right are separated by commas, top to bottom by dashes.

ACKNOWLEDGMENTS

The editors of this book are indebted to Dr. James F. Shearer, Professor of Spanish Literature, the Graduate Faculties, Columbia University; to Dr. René C. Taylor, Visiting Professor (1961-1962) in Art History and Archeology at Columbia University and formerly Professor at the University of Granada, Spain; and to Dr. Dante A. Puzzo, Associate Professor of History, The City University of New York—all of whom read and commented on portions of the text.

Index

This symbol in front of a page number indicates a photograph or painting of the subject mentioned.

XX

Production staff for Time Incorporated

John L. Hallenbeck (Vice President and Director of Production)

Robert E. Foy, Caroline Ferri and Robert E. Fraser

Text photocomposed under the direction of

Albert J. Dunn and Arthur J. Dunn